Hope

for the Broken Soul

ISBN: 9798753228208
Summit Global Publishing Ltd.
8717 50 St NW, Edmonton, AB, T6B1E7, tracy@thesummitchurch.ca
Edited by: Tracy Belford & Elizabeth Urban
Cover by Krysta Koppel
© Aleksey Popov Dreamstime.com
ID 177474048© Rszarvas Dreamstime.com ID 23713557

Bible References

The Amplified Bible. (1987). La Habra, CA: The Lockman Foundation. Used by Permission

The Holy Bible: King James Version. (1995). (electronic ed. of the 1769 edition of the 1611 Authorized Version., Ps 51:6). Bellingham WA: Logos Research Systems, Inc. Used by permission

The Holy Bible: New International Version. (1984). Grand Rapids, MI: Zondervan. Used by permission

The Passion Translation: New Testament. (2017). Simmons, B. (Trans.). BroadStreet Publishing. Used by permission

Hope

for the Broken Soul

By Louise M. Franck
hopeforthebrokensoul@gmail.com

Author of
You're all a Bunch of Peas

Contents

Dedication	1
Acknowledgements	2
To those who Co-Labour with me in ministry	3
To the Brave Warriors	4
My prayer for all of you	6
Endorsements	7
Foreword	10
Introduction	13
God's Original Plan for Man	16
The Greatest Gift of All	22
Jesus the Physician	28
True Peace and Joy	31
The Need for Spiritual Gifts	40
Come Out, Come Out Wherever You Are	43
Meditation and Our Mind	55
Hope for the Shattered Scriptures	61
Testimonies from Brokenness to Wholeness	66
My Own Journey	67
Brody's Journey	82
Kelly's Journey	88
John's Journey	96
Cindy's Journey	98
Sharon's Journey	103
Mary's Journey	107

Anna's Journey	112
Betsie's Journey	117
Veronica's Journey	119
The Prayer, Written by Lana Saretsky	122
My Life Before Jesus Christ	123
My New Life with Jesus Christ	136
Conclusion	146
Commentary on Noah's Ark, by Michelle McDonald	150
Other Books by the Same Author	156
Recommended Ministries	158
Recommended Material	159

Dedication

To all who have suffered neglect, trauma and abuse: my desire is to share the hope and the answers that bring healing and wholeness to your souls.

Acknowledgements

Michelle McDonald

I would like to thank Michelle McDonald for sharing "Commentary on Noah's Ark".

Michayla Taylor

I also would like to thank my granddaughter Michayla for writing the dedication for my book and rescuing me from my poor computer skills.

Jason Wiebe

I also want to thank Jason Wiebe for his help in editing as well.

Lana Saretsky

I would like to thank Lana for writing "The Prayer".

Andre and Linda Reijnders

I am grateful for all your loving support, encouragement, and intercession for this journey. Thank you for working on the editing, the technical support, and wonderful suggestions that helped write this book. God bless you both for your serving hearts. You have been an answer to my prayers and needs.

To those who Co-Labour with me in Ministry

I would first like to thank Tricia Betz, who ministers with me most of the time. You are so willing to pour yourself out for **Hope for the Broken Soul Ministries**. You are a mighty intercessor and leader. I am grateful for your willingness to travel with me and remind me of any changes in our schedule. Thank you for being a key part of the ministry and for your friendship, prayers, support, and encouragement that you always show me.

To Kimberley Stevens, Hans Stevens, Susan Miller, and Lee Miller: thank you so much for your leadership and faithfulness to minister to the broken and shattered souls God brings along our paths. Thank you for pouring your lives into all who long for wholeness. You are all amazing and I am honoured to minister with you all. Thank you for your love and support in the ministry God has called us to.

To The Brave Warriors

Thank you to those who were willing to share their testimonies of healing from brokenness; great is your reward. I know your testimonies will bring hope, healing, and understanding to many unanswered questions for those who have also suffered. Blessings and great rewards come to the humble and willing hearts who desire to share what God has done for them.

The Bible

"This book contains the mind of God, the state of man, the way of salvation, the doom of sinners, and the happiness of believers. Its doctrines are holy, its precepts are binding, its histories are true, and its decisions are immutable. Read it to be wise, believe it to be safe, and practice it to be holy. It contains light to direct you, food to support you, and comfort to cheer you. It is the traveller's map, the pilgrim's staff, the pilot's compass, the soldier's sword, and the Christian's charter. Here paradise is restored, heaven opened, and the gates of hell disclosed. Christ is its grand object, our good its design, and the glory of God its end. It should fill the memory, rule the heart, and guide the feet. Read it slowly, frequently, and prayerfully. It is a mine of wealth, a paradise of glory, and a river of pleasure. It is given to you in life, will be opened in the judgment, and will be remembered forever. It involves the highest responsibility, will reward the greatest labour, and will condemn all who trifle with its sacred contents."

Author unknown

My Prayer for all of you

Philippians 1:9-11 (NIV)

And this is my prayer: that your love may abound more and more in knowledge and depth of insight, so that you may be able to discern what is best and may be pure and blameless until the day of Christ, filled with the fruit of righteousness that comes through Jesus Christ - to the glory and praise of God.

Endorsements

I highly recommend this book, especially to those who have suffered from abuse, trauma, and neglect, as well as to those who minister to broken and shattered hearts. At first, I was skeptical about the process, but after seeing so many in the body of Christ being healed in areas of their lives, the positive results are undeniable. Wounded parts of our souls are touched by Jesus and healed. The evidence is restoration, integration and wholeness. This brings changes in behaviour, habits and freedom to pursue our calling in Jesus Christ. Louise Franck is a spiritually mature Christian leader with an anointing of the Holy Spirit in this ministry. She is transparent in sharing her personal journey of "been there" experiences. Louise loves God's presence and power and waits for His leading. Her life is under the Lordship of Jesus Christ. She is committed and dedicated to seeing others come to wholeness.

Tricia Betz Intercessor, Co-Minister

Hope for the Broken Soul Ministries

I was first introduced to the ministry of Hope for the Broken Soul eight years ago. My first experience in this area was when Louise asked me to come with her and record what was being said in her sessions. I agreed to be a support to my friend, despite being somewhat skeptical and having no idea of what to expect.

During the sessions, there were times as different parts would speak, that Louise's facial expressions might change, or the inflections of her voice would alter. I left those sessions knowing that this was a real experience, and that parts of Louise were receiving healing and integration.

For me, the proof of the pudding is in the eating. The biggest testimony to the validity of the ministry Louise was receiving was the change in her personality and how she did life. Louise was much calmer, and things did not so readily upset her. Even her thinking became clearer and making better decisions was easier as there were not so many distractions in her head.

Louise has changed chairs. Now she is ministering healing to others and people are being set free. I still pray and minister in sessions.

Through the grace of our mighty God, she now leads these sessions and is bringing people like me and you to freedom from events, traumas, and memories of our past. We all need to determine to change the chairs of our lives and move from victim to victor.

Susan Miller

Intercessor, co-Minister at Hope for the Broken Soul Ministry

I have known Louise for several years now and am excited to recommend this new book. I've seen firsthand the personal struggle she has gone through and her commitment to help others who are struggling with similar difficulties. Her ministry is essential to not only the body of Christ, but anyone who struggles in life because of traumas from their past. Her goal is to help set people free so that they can live their lives liberated from the effects of trauma. I am one that has been helped immensely through her ministry. I am pleased to recommend this book to anyone that does not want to continue to live the defeated life and be able to succeed in living the life that God has ordained for you. Allow God to minister to your soul as you read the different testimonies.

Hans Stevens

Lay Minister

Foreword

Dear Reader,

As the Church continues to move forward through time, we are getting closer to the eminent return of Jesus. How close that is I dare not say: however, no matter when, there is a growing sense that Jesus, through the Holy Spirit, is working at bringing healing and wholeness to His people. The ministry of the Messiah is to heal the broken hearted, set the captives free, and release prisoners from darkness. The Church is the extended hand of Jesus on the earth to do just that. The problem is that a lot of us in the church are just as broken and captive as those in the world. Jesus wants to and needs to change that, so we can become beacons of hope in the world.

In this book, Louise lays a foundation through Scripture and through her own testimony of her continuing walk to wholeness as well as her experience ministering to and helping others walk to wholeness and freedom. I have known Louise since 1998 and have witnessed the change in her life since she has been ministered to. I have also ministered with her to those who have sought wholeness, and have witnessed the dramatic changes in their lives as they faced the wounding of their past and received healing, integration, and at times deliverance from darkness. No two people are the same. It is a profound work of the Holy Spirit in each person's life and one by one, people are coming to wholeness.

One of the reasons for this book is for those who walk in a healing and deliverance ministry to have another helpful way to bring healing and wholeness to those they minister to. When one or two people minister to one person, it takes a long time. There are a lot of broken people out there who need this and use it as a vital tool in their ministry.

For those of you who have a mature walk with God, you may begin to recognize areas of your life that you've struggled with. With the Holy Spirit's help, you will recognize emotional triggers and begin integration on your own, but if it gets too discouraging or difficult, have someone like Louise walk with you through the process. As you experience wholeness and freedom you will have a testimony and can help others begin to walk in wholeness as well.

For those of you who are new believers, or new to this kind of ministry, I pray that God will show you the reality and validity of this type of ministry. It is through the power of God's written Word and the power of the Holy Spirit in us that we are saved, made whole, healed, delivered and set free! Seek God, press into Him, study the Bible and seek good fellowship. As you experience the power of God at work in your life bringing healing and wholeness, you too will have a testimony and the ability to be a minister of wholeness.

Lee Miller

Bachelor of Theology, Northwest Bible College

Fear not [there is nothing to fear], for I am with you; do not look around you in terror and be dismayed, for I am your God. I will strengthen and harden you to difficulties, yes, I will help you; yes, I will hold you up and retain you with My [victorious] right hand of rightness and justice. Isaiah 41:10 (Amplified)

Let your character or moral disposition be free from love of money [including greed, avarice, lust, and craving for earthly possessions] and be satisfied with your present [circumstances and with what you have]; for He [God] Himself has said, I will not in any way fail you nor give you up nor leave you without support. [I will] not, [I will] not, [I will] not in any degree leave you helpless nor forsake nor let [you] down (relax My hold on you)! [Assuredly not!] Hebrews 13:5 (Amplified)

He who gets wisdom loves his own soul; he who cherishes understanding prospers. Proverbs 19:8 (NIV)

A man's wisdom gives him patience; it is to his glory to overlook an offense. Proverbs 19:11 (NIV)

Introduction

Many people need healing from the brokenness of past neglect, trauma, and abuse- some more than others. God's Word tells us that if a house is divided against itself, it cannot stand. (Matthew 12:25) When our soul is divided, fragmented, splintered, in parts, broken, or shattered, we become double-minded and unstable in all our ways.

I am a miracle, as God has brought me out of a past of mental, physical, emotional, spiritual, and sexual abuse. I have never been on medications, in any kind of professional counselling, psychiatry, or therapy. Only God could have carried me through this life of pain, sorrow, and abuse. He healed me and made me whole.

God desires to bring all of humanity to healing and wholeness, so that we can love like He loves us. God is love; pure love and only love can mend a broken heart. In other words, only God's pure love can mend our broken hearts.

This book explains what happens to our soul, which consists of our mind, our emotions and our heart, in times of traumatic experiences. Included are personal testimonies from individuals who have lived with parts or triggers and have come through to the other side of healing and wholeness with God. These testimonies have been written in their own words.

*Behold, thou desirest truth in the inward **parts**: and in the hidden **part** thou shalt make me to know wisdom.*
Psalm 51:6 (KJV)

With the breakdown of marriages and families, the hearts of most are broken and growing colder. No one is able to heal in isolation. We need one another. This requires commitment, sacrifice, and dedicated love for the hurting souls that God brings along our path. When the very foundation of a soul, a society, or a nation is broken and separated from God, it becomes a perfect recipe for hell, death, and destruction in our everyday lives. God tells us that if we live by His Word, we are like a wise man who built his house on the rock. If we are like a house, and if Jesus is our rock, we will not fall. If we do not choose to live this way, the foundation of our lives will be like a house built on sinking sand. When the trials come, we will fall. (Matthew 7:24-27)

There are deep places of the soul where our pain and darkness have split off and are hidden away. We can also call "parts" or "split offs" the triggers in our lives. We need filters for a car, furnace or vacuums. When our hearts, emotions and minds have suffered traumas, abuse and neglect, the filters in our souls respond out of our wounds and past abuses and hurts easily trigger us. When past wounds or triggers are willing to be healed, we no longer respond to our past as we used to. It is by the gifts of the Holy Spirit, along with love, time, and patience that these broken and shattered souls can come to wholeness.

Many people suffer with overwhelming feelings of despair, hopelessness, loneliness, anger, and thoughts that life will never change. There is much pain in people sitting in the pews of the church. Many Christians walk into church on Sunday with their broken and shattered souls and leave the same way. As Christians, we often put on our Sunday faces and leave, pretending all is fine in our lives. It is time to be real and come together in love. We need to be willing to share our time and whatever else it takes, to see our brothers and sisters in Christ, as well as those who have yet to come to Him, to come to fullness in Him. This means laying down our lives for one another. We will hear one question when we arrive in heaven, **"Did you learn to love?"** Jesus tells us that the world will know us by our love for one another. (John 13:34-35)

Healing takes time and Jesus Christ knows the process for us to come to healing and wholeness. We need to realize that Jesus paid for every broken heart of mankind on the cross. During times of ministry, Jesus walks into the many parts that are broken, shattered, and living in the deep darkness of past traumas. Jesus comes with His love and sends the darkness running. Jesus is amazing; He knows what each part needs in order to come to freedom and wholeness.

God's Original Plan for Man

In The Beginning

The Book of Genesis speaks of God the Creator. He made the heavens and the earth. God created all things, including man and woman, whom He called Adam and Eve. God made mankind in His image and likeness. God also planted the Garden of Eden. He placed Adam and Eve there and supplied all their needs. Adam and Eve would walk and talk with God in the garden. They had a personal relationship with God Himself. Life was perfect in paradise. There was no pain, sorrow, abuse, loneliness, fear, or shame. There was only pure love and unspeakable joy and peace. They lived in perfect harmony with God. (Genesis 2:8–25)

In the middle of the garden there was a Tree of Life and a Tree of Knowledge of Good and Evil. God also gave Adam and Eve a free will. They could choose. God commanded Adam and Eve not to eat from the tree of knowledge of good and evil. God warned them if they did eat from this tree, they would die. (Genesis 3:1–24)

I understand Christians know what the Bible says, but there may be those who have never read the Bible and therefore I feel it is important to share these truths from God's Word.

The devil, as we know, came and deceived Adam and Eve. God had given Adam and Eve a precious gift. They had a choice to obey or disobey Him. Even after God's warning, they chose to listen to the enemy of their souls, the devil. Because they had sinned, they could no longer live in the Garden of Eden.

Sin cannot dwell in the Glory and Presence of God. (Genesis 3:8) Life as they knew it was over because sin had entered the world. The devil now had a right to come and steal, kill, or destroy anyone willing to listen to him. Good and evil are still in this world. We all still have a free will. We can choose to obey God or disobey Him. Even though man chose to disobey God, He demonstrates His great grace, mercy, and compassion for fallen man by sending a promised Saviour Jesus Christ. God sent Jesus, His Word, as a guide to know Him and walk in His wisdom.

*And then the lawless one will be revealed, whom the Lord Jesus will overthrow with the breath of his mouth and destroy by the splendor of his coming. The coming of the lawless one will be in accordance with the work of Satan displayed in all kinds of counterfeit miracles, signs and wonders, and in every sort of evil that deceives those who are perishing. They perish because they **refused** to love the **truth** and so be saved.*
2 Thessalonians 2:9-10 (NIV)

Since the beginning and until the end, man continues to have a free will to sin or to obey God. God loves us so much that He tells us what can harm us and what protects us. Truly, the only power the devil can have over us is when we are willing to believe his lies. Satan is the father of lies. (John 8:44). He will always try to twist the Word of God as he did with Adam and Eve in the Garden of Eden. God's Word is the Truth and it is His Truth that shall set us free from deception. God allows us to make our own choices; He has given us free will to listen or not to listen to His Wisdom and believe His Word. (Deuteronomy 30:11–20) We can choose to bring our pain, rejection, and abuse to Him or not to bring it. We can choose to sin in ways that will bring brokenness to ourselves and others. We can also choose to allow Jesus into our pain and traumas of the past so we can be healed and whole. When we are healed, we can become vessels of healing to others.

Life is all about choices, like how we will respond when we are hurt, wounded or wronged. Wounds of every kind can harm us from conception and throughout our lives. Sometimes it is not easy to make the right choice in times of abuse and trauma. We must all learn that God's great grace and mercy are always there to help us, heal us, protect us, and supply us with all of our needs. There will always be those who love their sin and desire to inflict pain and sorrow on others. Again, God will not force us to choose right from wrong. Who has not suffered from the words and actions of others? Terrible things can happen to us as babies, as little children and throughout our lives. Only Jesus knows who will come to Him and surrender their lives and sorrows to Him in order to receive healing and wholeness.

In the Book of Genesis, God tells us about Cain and Abel. Abel kept flocks and Cain worked the soil. Abel offered to God the best of his flock, while Cain brought only some of the fruits of the soil. God was pleased with Abel's offering. Cain's offering did not receive favor from God. God in His grace told him if he did what was right, he too would receive favor. God warned Cain that sin was standing right at his door, wanting to have him. God told Cain he had to master sin. (Genesis 4:1-7) Our battle always begins in our mind. We must choose not to sin and be quick to draw close to God, resist that devil, and when we do, he must leave us. (James 4:7) This is a daily battle till the end. We all make choices in life to forgive or not to forgive. (Matthew 6:14-15) I know this is not an easy thing to do when there has been great betrayal, abuse, or neglect. If we are willing to give Jesus our pain, fears, anger, hatred, unforgiveness, rejections, neglect, and sins, then He comes and begins the healing. Because God gave us free will, He still requires our permission to come into our hearts and places of great sorrow and darkness.

The enemy of our souls will do all he can do to hinder our good choices. It has taken me a life time to wake up, let go, and let God come in and heal my brokenness and take away my shame. As I experience Jesus' healing touch, I only wish I would have made the good choices to forgive and let go a long time ago. I pray and hope by sharing my journey as well as the journeys of others, many will choose to allow Jesus entry into their hidden places of brokenness and darkness.

The Lord once told me everything is a choice in life. Forgiveness removes the triggers that cause pain to us and others. As I surrender the triggers, splinters, and fragments from past fears and abuse, I am not only healed, but God gives me His love for others so I can pray for their salvation and healing. This does not mean I need to associate with them when they are still not safe, but I can pray from a distance. There have been times when I have had encounters with some who abused me or my family, only to find out the depth of my healing. I was surprised that there were no bad feelings, just compassion for their broken lives. We can never justify sin, but when we are healed, the sin of another cannot touch or trigger us anymore. In my testimony I share how the triggers or parts were actually parts of me that had split off. Some were parts trapped in great fear; others were angry and could be violent. Many parts of me would split off at a time, depending on the circumstance.

When you choose to forgive, that is true and complete healing. That is the great life changing power, when we choose to forgive and love.

Despite it taking years to forgive them, when I did, my healing came quickly. I would persevere and say to God, "I choose to forgive and bless them. Change my heart and heal me." I would also pray for that person and ask God to save, heal and bless them. That is exactly what would happen. God healed me and changed my heart. There are times when relationships that are broken because of trauma and abuse, can be restored. This can only happen because of God's amazing love for humanity. (John 3:16) God's Word tells us to live in peace whenever possible. (Romans 12:18, 2 Corinthians 13:11 and 1 Thessalonians 5:13)

The Greatest Gift of All

Love came down from heaven to rescue humanity. God's greatest gift to humanity is sending His one and only Son, Jesus Christ, to die and pay the highest price for all the sins, pain, sorrows, and sicknesses of mankind. (John 3:16)

Who has believed our message and to whom has the arm of the LORD been revealed? He grew up before him like a tender shoot, and like a root out of dry ground. He had no beauty or majesty to attract us to him, nothing in his appearance that we should desire him. He was despised and rejected by men, a man of sorrows, and familiar with suffering. Like one from whom men hide their faces he was despised, and we esteemed him not. Surely he took up our infirmities and carried our sorrows, yet we considered him stricken by God, smitten by him, and afflicted. But he was pierced for our transgressions, he was crushed for our iniquities; the punishment that brought us peace was upon him, and by his wounds we are healed. We all, like sheep, have gone astray, each of us has turned to his own way; and the LORD has laid on him the iniquity of us all. He was oppressed and afflicted, yet he did not open his mouth; he was led like a lamb to the slaughter, and as a sheep before her shearers is silent, so he did not open his mouth. By oppression and judgment he was taken away. And who can speak of his descendants? For he was cut off from the land of the living; for the transgression of my people he was stricken. He was assigned a grave with the wicked, and with the rich in his death, though he had done no violence, nor was any deceit in his mouth. Yet it was the LORD's will to crush him and cause him to suffer, and though the LORD makes his life a guilt offering, he will see his offspring and prolong his days, and the will of the LORD will prosper in his hand. After the suffering of his soul, he will see the light of life and be satisfied; by his knowledge my righteous servant will justify many, and he will bear their iniquities. Therefore I will give him a portion among the great, and he will divide the spoils with the strong, because he poured out his life unto death, and was numbered with the transgressors. For he bore the sin of many, and made intercession for the transgressors. Isaiah 53 (NIV)

Just before Jesus took His last breath, He declared, "It is finished." (John 19:30) He paid it all, once for all.

God desires to pour out His mercy, peace and love in abundance into our lives. If we will invite God into the pain and traumas of our lives, we increasingly come to understand how high, long, wide, and deep His love is for us. (Ephesians 3:18-19) Each person I have ministered to had big issues of trust. Many are so angry with God and blame Him for not stopping the pain and sorrows in their lives. I must explain to all these parts that God will not come against anyone's free will. I also tell them they have a right to be angry, but they must come to a place of forgiveness. This takes time and often many sessions before they are willing to do this.

I must tell anyone who reads this book, "God has so much love and patience with the parts of our souls that are still in pieces."

I tell these parts God can be trusted and has only goodness in store for them. When they finally surrender to Him, they always find healing and freedom for the first time in their lives. They always cry tears of joy and experience great relief from all the burdens they have carried in order to survive.

Something I have also learned about parts is that the enemy of our soul will always attack our gifts and calling on our lives. If you are anointed to write songs and lead worship, for instance, he will do all he can to ensure you never fulfill your destiny as a worship leader. The devil knows our gifts and will always use the traumas and pain in our lives to say we have no future. If we are willing to surrender our lives and allow Jesus to heal us, we will most certainly fulfill the call on our lives.

God calls us a chosen people, a royal priesthood, a holy nation, a people belonging to God that we may declare the praises of Him who called us out of darkness into His glorious light. (1 Peter 2:9)

God has given some to be apostles, some to be prophets, some to be evangelists, some to be pastors, and and some to be teachers in order to prepare the people of God for works of service. (Ephesians 4:11) These callings are needed in order that the Body of Christ be built up and come to unity in the faith in the knowledge of the Son of God. This is so that we may become mature and come to fullness in Jesus Christ. Some have been called to business, to the medical field, to politics, or to research, and the list goes on. The enemy wants to sabotage our future by keeping us trapped in the broken and shattered places of our soul.

The more we desire healing, the better we are equipped to leave the elementary teaching about Christ and go on in maturity. God is gracious and compassionate as He waits for us to let go of our past and allow Him in our hearts, so we can experience a deeper walk with Him. When our hearts are broken, Jesus' work in our lives is limited. We cannot fully walk with God, whilst we hold onto pain and trauma. Everyone who is willing to invite Jesus into their hidden places of pain and fear will experience His great love and compassion. They fall more in love with Him and are never the same.

When we are broken, our relationships suffer and those around us suffer as well. As you read the testimonies in this book, you will understand the power of forgiveness and letting go of our past so we can move on into the future God has for us. I pray the testimonies speak for themselves.

*:14 For if you **forgive** people their trespasses [their reckless and willful sins, leaving them, letting them go, and giving up resentment], your heavenly Father will also forgive you.*
*:15 But if you do not **forgive** others their trespasses [their reckless and willful sins, leaving them, letting them go, and*

giving up resentment], neither will your Father forgive you your trespasses.   Matthew 6:14-15 (Amplified)

God can heal our broken hearts and bring us to wholeness. Jesus waits for anyone who is willing to come to Him for healing. He has been waiting for some people for sixty plus years. Truly, He is patient and desires that no one die in the traumas of the past since He paid for all our sins and sufferings.

This ministry is truly a gift from God to anyone who would put their trust in Him alone for healing and wholeness. To all who are hidden in spiritual pits, prisons and dungeons of the soul, "Come to Jesus". Even now at this moment you can ask Jesus to forgive you of your sins and come into your brokenness. Ask Him to be your Lord. Even if you're afraid to speak this, you can say these words in your heart so the enemy cannot hear you and Jesus will come and rescue you.

I also want to tell your parts that are Protectors that have been taking care of many others, "All of you, come to Jesus together, to be healed. If one of you can speak for all of you, pray and ask Jesus to forgive all your sins and be your Lord." He will come and bring forgiveness and healing and wholeness.

Jesus has great and immense love, healing, and deliverance for everyone. You never need to be broken and shattered again. He desires you be whole and one with Him.

I bless each of your parts with His love. Come! He has been waiting for you with arms wide open. This is the desire of God's heart for all who are caught in lies and traps of the past.

*A psalm of David. The L*ORD *is my shepherd, I shall not be in want. He makes me lie down in green pastures, he leads me beside quiet waters, he restores my soul. He guides me in paths of righteousness for his name's sake. Even though I walk through the valley of the shadow of death, I will fear no evil, for you are with me; your rod and your staff, they comfort me. You prepare a table before me in the presence of my enemies. You anoint my head with oil; my cup overflows. Surely goodness and love will follow me all the days of my life, and I will dwell in the house of the L*ORD *forever.*

Psalm 23 (NIV)

*Praise be to the L*ORD*, for he has heard my cry for mercy. The L*ORD *is my strength and my shield; my heart trusts in him, and I am helped. My heart leaps for joy and I will give thanks to him in song. The L*ORD *is the strength of his people, a fortress of salvation for his anointed one. Save your people and bless your inheritance; be their shepherd and carry them forever.*

Psalm 28:6-9 (NIV)

Jesus the Physician

Jesus came to heal all that has been lost and stolen from our lives. He is after our hearts. He is a God who desires a personal relationship with all of us. He is not interested in lip service or religious rituals made by man. He made us and died for our sins and brokenness. He came to pay the price for sin, pain, sickness, and all the sorrows of mankind. His death on the Cross is His greatest gift of love we could ever receive. He is not mad at us and He is not disappointed with us. He is full of grace and mercy, standing with His arms wide open, saying, "Come to Me and let Me heal you."

God says He has wonderful plans for all of us. He desires to give us all a hope and future. (Jeremiah 29:11) The Cross is the only answer for our healing. This is something I share with the unhealed parts of those I pray with for healing. We must allow Jesus to rebuild the broken foundations of our souls. When Jesus comes into the places of trauma, abuse or neglect, He can and will bring you out healed and whole.

I know this as truth, as He has walked with me back into my past. Jesus brings great healing and joy. Jesus has also been with me in these times of abuse, even if I did not know it at the time. When parts of me are willing to come and embrace Jesus and allow Him to heal me, the parts or triggers of my past come to a place of deeper wholeness. The process for wholeness takes time and when wounds are deep, we need to trust God with the healing process. I once asked God if I could minister to someone who I knew was broken and shattered. God told me, "Not at this time", as she was not ready. He showed me a picture of removing a scab before a wound was healed, made the wound bleed more and the scar bigger. We need the Holy Spirit to guide and counsel us for everyone's healing.

I was angry with God for many years, wondering where He was in these terrible times of my life. Why did He not stop the abuse from happening? God reminded me that every person has a free will. He will not take that away from us. Since the beginning of time Jesus has known all our imperfections. He knows everything we will walk through in our lives. He knows everything from the beginning till the end of our lives. He knows all our thoughts and all the choices that we will make in this life. I encourage everyone to read and meditate on the Book of John, and to read it often, asking the Holy Spirit to reveal how high, long, wide, and deep the love of God is for humanity. (Ephesians 3:18) There are times when we do not see justice done here on earth. There is a day when all humanity will stand before the God of Justice, Jesus Christ, and justice will be served. (Matthew 25: 31-46) Those who have repented during their lives here on earth will live and reign with Jesus Christ forever. This will be a time for great rejoicing forever and forever. Those who have refused to forgive and reject the cross of Jesus Christ will receive God's justice. This will be a place of eternal darkness and great suffering that will never end.

True Peace and Joy

There is a high price to be paid to attain maturity. We are justified through our faith, which brings peace with God, through Jesus Christ. We have all met folks who walk in maturity and those who do not. Maturity really comes most often through the things we suffer. God's Word tells us that suffering produces perseverance which leads to building character and hope. (Romans 5:3-5) There are so many stories in the Bible of men and women who have braved the difficult times in their lives. Not one of these folks could have come through their times of suffering unless they were willing to be courageous and persevere. Because of their choices, they became men and women of strength, character, and valour.

The Book of James tells us that our faith will be tested as we face trials of many kinds. (James 1:2-5) Regardless of whether we are Christians or not, we will all be tested through the trials of our lives. God says that perseverance must finish its work in order for us to attain maturity. History gives great honour to those who, through the testing of their faith and persistence, became very effective and productive people who changed the world for good and the Glory of God.

God's Word also encourages us to make every effort to add to our faith that which is beneficial, sound information, self-control, and the most important, which is brotherly kindness and love. (2 Peter 1:5-8) The Word of God tells us if we increase in these qualities, we will have productive lives as we increase in our knowledge of our Lord Jesus Christ

God promises that if we choose to walk in His ways, we will not fall and will receive a rich welcome when we meet Him face to face. Before I made the choice to believe and trust Jesus Christ with my life, I was consumed with the pain, sorrows, fears, and sin in my life. Not until I looked up and cried for help from Jesus Christ, did my life begin to change. For the rest of my life, as I walk with my King, I must daily choose to keep my eyes on Him alone, not on my circumstances. Our faith must be in Jesus Christ and not in the outcome of our circumstances or prayers.

He has already overcome all I will ever face, because He went ahead of me and paid the price for my sins and healing at Calvary. He is the one who supplies all of my needs daily and will continue to do so until the end. (Philippians 4:19) As Jesus walks me through healing and the refining fires of my life, I am finding true joy and peace for my soul. I know that I know that He is always with me, guiding me, providing for me, and helping me with every step I take with Him. In the past, the pain in my life and the pain in others around me would clash and cause a bigger mess. As I am still in the process of being healed, I see those broken around me with greater love and compassion. True joy and peace come from knowing Jesus and having a healed heart. The broken pieces of my life are now healing and I am becoming more and more one in my heart, mind and soul. Wow! What joy and freedom!!

The Apostle Paul prays:

I pray that out of his glorious riches he may strengthen you with power through his Spirit in your inner being, so that Christ may dwell in your hearts through faith. And I pray that you, being rooted and established in love, may have power, together with all the saints, to grasp how wide and long and high and deep is the love of Christ, and to know this love that surpasses knowledge—that you may be filled to the measure of all the fullness of God. Ephesians 3:16-19 (NIV)

God wants us to come to a place where we are complete in Him, not broken and shattered. If we willingly open up to God's love and healing touch, then we can grow in the fruit of the Holy Spirit.

But the fruit of the Spirit is love, joy, peace, patience, kindness, goodness, faithfulness, gentleness and self-control. Against such things there is no law. Galatians 5:22-23 (NIV)

Just as with little children growing up, life is all about them so many of us grow up and remain like little children. Life becomes all about us. We become selfish and place unreasonable demands on others. Then we wonder why we are so unhappy and why people avoid us. In life we are going to be either givers or takers. Life is a choice; we can refuse to change and not reach out for help. I have also met some who ask for prayer, but come with a long list of what they want God to do for them. No one tells God what to do. We must be willing to humble ourselves and submit our will to God's will. Even Jesus prayed in the Garden of Gethsemane, "not my will but Your will be done." (Luke 22:42) Why? God has the answers that will meet all of our needs. It is not easy to release full control of our lives to God, but as we humble ourselves before Him, He will bring healing and wholeness to our broken lives.

There are a lot of people who remain self-centered, but there are so many others who love and care. They are willing to go the extra mile to see wholeness come to the broken and shattered. If we choose to walk in a holy reverential fear of God, living in His presence and Word, sin will not control us. We must choose to keep our tongues from evil and speaking lies. We must choose to turn from evil and do what is good. If we want peace, we need to seek and pursue it. (1 Peter 3:10-11) God hears all our cries and He is always ready to help us. God also tells us His face is against those who do evil and will cut off the memory of them from the earth. (Psalm 34:16) When we as His children cry out to Jesus, He hears and delivers us from all our troubles. (Psalm 50:15) God tells us He is close to the broken hearted and will save us when our heart becomes crushed. (Psalm 34:18) Jesus promises us that when life is more than we can handle, He will provide a way of escape, revive us, and restore joy to our hearts. (1 Corinthians 10:13)

God's Word tells us that His love and faithfulness meet together; that righteousness and peace kiss each other. (Psalm 85:10) It is also written that a heart at peace gives life to the body, but if we choose to walk in jealousy, it will rot our bones. (Proverbs 14:30) If we are determined to take captive our thoughts and line them up to the Word of God, we will be kept in perfect peace. (Isaiah 26:3) I have found that to stay strong in my faith, I need to surround myself with Christians who are strong in their faith. (Hebrews 10:24-25) I have looked for those who are also safe and trustworthy as I submit to their wisdom and correction. Reading the Word daily, living in His presence, praying, worshipping, and fellowshipping are all necessary to stay strong in our faith. These are also the days when Christians need to meet often in worship, prayer, and sincere fellowship in order to stay strong.

As a side note, I encourage anyone who has suffered trauma in their lives to watch one of the best movies ever made, **Unbroken** *(2014)*, directed by Angelina Jolie. This is a true story of survival, resilience, and redemption. It is about the life of Olympian and war hero Louie Zamperini. This should have been Best Picture for the year. It is a difficult movie to watch, but there are great lessons one can learn from the choices Louie Zamperini made. His choice to forgive brought him healing and freedom from his tormentors. There is nothing God cannot do for us if we will allow Him into our hearts and sorrows.

I receive many phone calls as an intercessor. There are times when I am having a difficult time when these calls come, but I put aside my need and pray with others. Then I end up ministering to myself at the same time. During these times, I pray the Word of God and in the Spirit, the gift of tongues, our heavenly language. In this way the Lord ministers to both of us.

But mark this: There will be terrible times in the last days. People will be lovers of themselves, lovers of money, boastful, proud, abusive, disobedient to their parents, ungrateful, unholy, without love, unforgiving, slanderous, without self-control, brutal, not lovers of the good, treacherous, rash, conceited, lovers of pleasure rather than lovers of God— having a form of godliness but denying its power. Have nothing to do with them.   2 Timothy 3:1-5 (NIV)

We have all experienced wounds and believed lies about ourselves and others. God's Word tells us that if we persevere in the trials of life and testing of our faith, we will receive the crown of life that God has promised to those of us who love Him. God's Word describes temptations as well.

Blessed is the man who perseveres under trial, because when he has stood the test, he will receive the crown of life that God has promised to those who love him. When tempted, no one should say, "God is tempting me." For God cannot be tempted by evil, nor does he tempt anyone; but each one is tempted when, by his own evil desire, he is dragged away and enticed. Then, after desire has conceived, it gives birth to sin; and sin, when it is full-grown, gives birth to death.

James 1:12-15 (NIV)

Now that is food for thought. Truly the battles of our lives begin in our minds. God warns us to take our thoughts captive. (2 Corinthians 10:3–5) If our minds are fixed on God and His Word, we will walk in peace through any situation. There is an old saying, "Practice makes perfect". Taking our thoughts captive is something we must practice daily - sometimes moment by moment. Peace that goes beyond human understanding comes only through knowing the one true God, Jesus Christ. Peace according to the world is living a life without trouble. You can have all the money you need, you can have your health, your family can be doing well, etc. All this is good, but life here is only for a season.

We all know life on this earth with or without Jesus will never be perfect, let alone be a paradise. A life fixed on Jesus can live in peace in the midst of any kind of storm that life may bring. The peace I am talking about is when all hell breaks loose in your life and you can stand with peace in your heart, knowing that Jesus is carrying you and will bring you through it all. His love for us becomes the strength of our heart, and our help in and through all things that come our way. There are times in our walk with God, when we experience hurts and struggles. In these times the enemy of our soul comes and tries to divide and break our relationships. When wounds are deep, we need to fight our negative thoughts that would play right into the hands of our enemy, who is standing at the door of our hearts, ready to take us captive to sin.

Our soul consists of our mind - what we reason or think; our will - what we decide or want; and our emotions - what we feel.

God desires to give us both physical and emotional healing, as well as deliver us from the root of bitterness. (Hebrews 12:15) A healed soul is a joyful soul. Nehemiah 8:10b tells us that the joy of the Lord is our strength.

And may the God of peace Himself sanctify you through and through [separate you from profane things, make you pure and wholly consecrated to God]; and may your **spirit and soul and body** *be preserved sound and complete [and found] blameless at the coming of our Lord Jesus Christ (the Messiah).*

1 Thessalonians 5:23 (Amplified)

You will guard him and keep him in perfect and constant peace whose **mind** *[both its inclination and its character] is stayed on You, because he commits himself to You, leans on You, and hopes confidently in You.* Isaiah 26:3 (Amplified)

For the god of this world has blinded the unbelievers' **minds** *[that they should not discern the truth], preventing them from seeing the illuminating light of the Gospel of the glory of Christ (the Messiah), Who is the Image and Likeness of God.*
2 Corinthians 4:4 (Amplified)

The Need for Spiritual Gifts

In 1 Corinthians 12:1-20 the Scripture talks about the gifts of the Holy Spirit. This Scripture also talks about the church being one Body, many parts.

There are different kinds of gifts, but the same Spirit. There are different kinds of service, but the same Lord. There are different kinds of working, but the same God works all of them in all men. Now to each one the manifestation of the Spirit is given for the common good.　　　　1 Corinthians 12:4-7 (NIV)

Every person on earth has been given gifts from God. No one is left out. The gifts are given for the common good. We can use our gifts as God directs and bring glory to His Name. We can also turn to the dark side and use the gifts God has given us for evil. God's Word tells us to follow the way of love and desire the spiritual gifts. During ministry time I often quietly pray in tongues, a spiritual language. This is perfect prayer and is wonderful when you are not sure what is going on. After praying, the Holy Spirit will show me what to say or do. I could never minister without the gifts of the Holy Spirit.

God's Word tells us these gifts are given to help us with works of service, so that the Body of Christ may be built up until we all reach unity in the faith and in the knowledge of the Son of God and become mature, attaining to the whole measure of the fullness of Christ. When God's people heal and come to wholeness, then we can walk in true love and unity.

If you have any encouragement from being united with Christ, if any comfort from his love, if any fellowship with the Spirit, if any tenderness and compassion, then make my joy complete by being like-minded, having the same love, being one in spirit and purpose. Do nothing out of selfish ambition or vain conceit, but in humility consider others better than yourselves. Each of you should look not only to your own interests, but also to the interests of others. Your attitude should be the same as that of Christ Jesus: Philippians 2:1-5 (NIV)

Most people are broken and shattered - some more than others. God is in a hurry to heal His people and see the church come to the fullness of Jesus Christ. This can only happen if we will allow Jesus into our hidden places of darkness. We must be willing to come into the fires of refining and not shrink back.

I see so many leaving the fellowship of believers out of frustration, because of offense, unforgiveness, and yes, even abuse. Truly, these are the days to seek God for healing and wholeness so we can fulfill the call of God on our lives. All I see in these ministry times are folks coming away healed and whole, walking in joy and freedom like never before. Jesus will never have you relive the abuse or pain; He wants to heal you and make you whole. I hope as you read the stories of others, you will see the need for healing from past traumas. Because I wish to be whole, I trust God to bring the healing I need in His time and His way. I will only see perfection, or being complete, when I meet Jesus face to face. I have asked Jesus to take all of me. I also know this is a process. If I am willing to surrender all to Jesus, He will bring me to wholeness and take me from strength to strength and glory to glory.

Come Out, Come Out Wherever You Are

An offended brother is more unyielding than a fortified city, and disputes are like the barred gates of a citadel.
                                        Proverbs 18:19 (NIV)

he is a double-minded man, unstable in all he does.
                                        James 1:8 (NIV)

The Hebrew word translated for offended means to break away. James 1:8 uses the Greek word *dipsuchos (dip'-soo-khos)* for double-minded, meaning to be two-spirited or vacillating in opinion or purpose.

When a person is traumatized, abused, or neglected, their mind can shut out the memory of these events and become parts. There can also be other parts that have different functions in their lives. There can be a part who is married, the one who goes to work, the one who is the parent, the one who deals with difficult situations or the one who goes to church and so on. Growing up, I developed different parts or roles in order to cope with the traumas of my life. The Word tells us when we ask God for wisdom or direction, we must believe God will help us and not fall into doubt or unbelief. (James 1:5-7)

If we doubt, are double-minded or wavering, the Word says we will be unstable in all our ways. (James 1:8) The Greek word translated for unstable *akatastatos (ak-at-as-tat-os)* means instability, disorder, commotion, confusion, tumult. (James 3:8) The Word also talks about our tongues. Our tongue is a small part of our body but our words, according to the book of James, can also be a fire, a world of evil. (James 3:5-6) We can completely corrupt our lives and others by the words we speak. Our words can bless or curse ourselves and others. We must take our thoughts captive, be quick to listen, and slow to speak. If we remain broken and shattered, how can we be single minded? When we are double minded, it is impossible to take our thoughts captive.

When a glass vase falls to the ground, it breaks into many pieces. The same can happen to our souls when there has been trauma, abuse, or neglect. Dr. Caroline Leaf PhD specializes in understanding how to get rid of our toxic thoughts and emotions based on biblical principles. After reading my book, I recommend Dr. Caroline Leaf's teaching called **Your Body His Temple: God's Plan for Achieving Emotional Wholeness.**

Our brains can be compared to an archive or register. We all have so much stored away, much like a filing system. There are times and events in our memory that, because of trauma, abuse, and neglect, have been archived and filed away, out of sight and out of mind. Then when something is said or done, a part that is still stuck in the past is triggered. Often these parts have different names, or they are called by certain emotions or functions. As an example, I will share in my testimony about my parts. There are many of us who have suffered trauma. I have met very few folks who have not suffered abuse, neglect, or trauma. Many of these events have kept us hidden away, trapped in pits, or hidden away in the prisons of our souls. Those of us who have suffered this way may not even be aware that we have split off. Through my healing journey I have become aware of my parts that were still trapped and hidden away. We often learn at a very young age, perhaps even as babies, to allow our souls to be split apart.

I experienced this during my healing sessions. Parts of me were still a baby or toddler. I recall a lady telling me when she was being abused, she would split off in her mind and go into the lampshade by the bed. This way she would not suffer the abuse. Another part of her took the abuse. There are parts that have no memory, but there are also parts that carry the memory for those who cannot handle the abuse. This is also a way to survive when life is unbearable. I can say these things, as I have lived this way and thank God for healing me more and more. I have also had people tell me they have no memory of their childhood. That can be a red flag. This may indicate that their soul parts have separated themselves from difficult events of the past. Jesus wants to take us to those places and heal us.

:17 And you, son of man, set your face against the daughters of your people who prophesy out of [the wishful thinking of] their own minds and hearts; prophesy against them,

:18 And say, Thus says the Lord God: Woe to the women who sew pillows to all armholes and fasten magic, protective charms to all wrists, and deceptive veils upon the heads of those of every stature to hunt and capture human lives! Will you snare the lives of My people to keep your own selves alive?

:19 You have profaned Me among My people [in payment] for handfuls of barley and for pieces of bread, slaying persons who should not die and giving [a guaranty of] life to those who should not live, by your lying to My people, who give heed to lies.

:20 Therefore thus says the Lord God: Behold, I am against your pillows and charms and veils with which you snare human lives like birds, and I will tear them from your arms and will let the lives you hunt go free, the lives you are snaring like birds.

:21 Your [deceptive] veils also will I tear and deliver My people out of your hand, and they shall be no more in your hand to be hunted and snared. Then you shall know (understand and realize) that I am the Lord.

:22 Because with lies you have made the righteous sad and disheartened, whom I have not made sad or disheartened, and because you have encouraged and strengthened the hands of

the wicked, that he should not return from his wicked way and be saved [in that you falsely promised him life],

:23 Therefore you will no more see false visions or practice divinations, and I will deliver My people out of your hand. Then you will know (understand and realize) that I am the Lord.
Ezekiel 13:17-23 (Amplified)

Wherefore thus saith the Lord GOD; Behold, I am against your pillows, wherewith ye there hunt the souls to make them fly, and I will tear them from your arms, and will let the souls go, even the souls that ye hunt to make them fly.
Ezekiel 13:20 (KJV)

The Hebrew word for fly is *parach (paw-rakh)* meaning to break, to fly, to scatter.

Also, in Jesus' Beatitudes' teaching in Matthew 5:3 (NIV) "Blessed are the poor in spirit", the Greek word translated for poor, *ptochos (pto-khos),* can mean causing the soul to fly away; to scare, to frighten. It can also mean a beggar.

Ezekiel 13:17-20 talks about witchcraft and how different cults can cause the soul to fly away, split off or become parts. Separation can happen in the womb and often within the early years of life.

My brokenness started in the first year of my life. Once a person experiences separation, they can do this all their life. How one does this, I do not know. I cannot explain this, but I know the human mind is amazing. Wicked people know how to traumatize someone and cause their minds to split off or fly away, and then control these parts of their lives. I can speak about such things as I was a victim of witchcraft.

Causing the soul to fly is a word that describes the fragmented soul. The same method is used when small children are expected to become soldiers. They traumatize the child by forcing them to kill someone. Their captors then control the parts that split off. Jesus came to open the blind eyes of those who are trapped in the traumas of their past and bring healing and wholeness.

Surely you desire truth in the inner parts; you teach me wisdom in the inmost place. Psalm 51:6 (NIV)

Behold, thou desirest truth in the inward parts: and in the hidden part thou shalt make me to know wisdom. Psalm 51:6 (KJV)

The Hebrew translation for hidden part is *satham*. It means: to stop up; to keep secret, closed up, hidden, secret, shut out (up), stop, to hide (by covering), literally or figuratively be absent, keep close, conceal, hide (self), (keep) secret, hidden. This gives us a clear picture what the soul can do under terrible circumstances. Some may find what I share about parts or triggers hard to believe, but God keeps those who are broken hearted close to His heart and those whose spirits have been crushed. (Psalms 34:18) God's Word tells us our spirit man keeps a record of our thoughts. (Malachi 3:16 and Hebrews 4:12) The Word also tells us that the Spirit of God searches all things, even the deep things of God. (1 Corinthians 2:10)

I have come to understand why I have not been able to recall some past events or even missing short periods of time previously. Now I realize it was because of the traumas of my past. There are also times when I was told, "You said and did such and such" and I would say "I did not". The reason I did not recall this, was that another part of me said and did such and such. I have experienced memories and flashbacks that brought back pictures of abuse. I have lost time because of never ending thoughts going on in my mind. I have experienced difficulty finding things or finding where I parked my car. That is so annoying! Sometimes I just have to laugh, otherwise I would start crying. I realize that when we are stressed, we can forget things, and this can be normal. I am not talking about that- what I am talking about is when this becomes a way of life. There were times when my mood suddenly switched. I have found I could remember a difficult circumstance, but at the same time separate myself from the emotion and physical pain. Although I know what happened, the circumstance could not have an effect on me.

I have also had parts that would show up and I would find myself in depression or hopelessness and deep fear. Other indications of being broken and shattered may be when a person goes for prayer over and over for the same thing and nothing ever changes. The same can happen in deliverance, if nothing ever changes. I understand that for some, after much prayer for healing and freedom, their lives still did not change. Other times, what appears to be a demon, is actually a part that needs love and deep healing. We truly need the leading of the Holy Spirit during ministry sessions.

Over the last few years, I have received much healing and wholeness. Once again, I thank the Pastors that God brought into my life, and for their twenty years of experience in dealing with the broken and shattered, and bringing healing to my life and many others. As I mentioned before, God has let me know the winter of my past abuse is over. Those who know me see so much more joy and peace in my life. Praise God, I can find my car now without it taking a half hour. That was not fun on a cold winter day.

In the pages ahead I will share some of my own ministry time and what Jesus did for me. For the other testimonies, the names of those people have been changed to protect their privacy. The testimonies will be in their own words. Through the ministry of **Hope for the Broken Soul**, God has brought many others, who have been broken and shattered, to a place of healing from their past wounds. Some of what you will read may surprise you. We have put God into a box along with our own ideas of how He will bring healing to our brokenness. God's Word tells us to look at the fruit produced in a person's life, and that would include a ministry as well.

When someone arrives for ministry, I have no idea what their need is. I have no idea what parts may be there. Prayer and inviting the Holy Spirit for wisdom and counsel is the only way to bring healing and wholeness to a broken and shattered soul. Most of the time God will show me their parts, that is, I see them in the spirit, or I have a vision or a thought. Sometimes God gives me a song to play that will bring a part up for healing. Other times God gives me the name of whole groups and they come for healing. There are also other times I play soaking (anointed instrumental) music. I then feel a strong presence of the Holy Spirit come into the room. There are times that the anointing on me is so strong that I must lay hands on the person, and God does His sovereign work in them. I simply wait for God to show me what my part is and then He does the healing. There are times I see a person's eyes or body language change as a sign that a part has come up to speak, or for healing. When I say I speak to parts, it simply means parts of the mind that are still trapped in a memory of the past.

There are times their voice will change and sound like a small child, or their tone of voice can change. This is also something I experienced during my own ministry times. I would feel like a little child and my voice would sound like a three-year-old. I also had a part that was a male part. My voice would change, because that part of me had to be strong and tough to deal with abuse and trauma. When I minister to others, I do not need to know all God is doing. I just need to obey what He is telling me or showing me to do. Every ministry time is different. That is why I need to hear from the Holy Spirit and follow His direction. The praise reports I hear after praying for the broken and shattered demonstrates the love and power of Jesus Christ, the comfort of the Holy Spirit, and our Heavenly Father's loving arms around His hurting children.

There are also parts of a person that can take on the role of a protector, watchman, or wall. In my journey I share about my parts as a protector or a wall. The wall is a part that stops access to any parts from coming up for healing. The protector does exactly what the Word says, protects parts that cannot deal with difficult situations. These are not demons but parts of the soul that rise up to help other parts that are trapped and unable to help themselves in times of trouble. There are times when a demon is attached to a part. When the enemy hinders a part from coming to Jesus, I ask the part that wants Jesus to simply ask Jesus, "Remove my enemies". There are other times when Jesus will tell me what to do concerning the enemy. When a part is willing to repent and receive Jesus as Lord and Saviour, the enemy loses his rights and must leave. There are also parts that can become very angry and frustrated with other parts. I had some very angry parts that could be easily triggered.

Some people may have a handful of parts while others may have thousands. There are people in government, doctors, judges, lawyers, movie stars, the rich and famous, leaders in the church, etc., who are broken and shattered. I once heard a Hollywood star say in an interview on TV, that it is one of her parts who want to perform. She is really shy, and in order to perform, she has another part that comes up to act, sing and dance. She even had a name for this part.

There is hope for all who are broken and shattered and who remain trapped in events of the past.

This is just a short explanation of being broken and shattered. When there is great fear, neglect, and trauma, our mind is well able to switch off or choose not to remember what has happened, and therefore splits off, splinters, flies away, becomes broken, and shattered into pieces. Once again, I mention at the end of my book some great reading that goes into an in-depth explanation about inner parts of the broken and shattered soul.

My biggest reason for writing this book is that through reading the testimonies, many will realize there is hope for those who suffer this way. Some of what you will read, as I said before, may seem strange or some may sound unbelievable.

All I can say is, let the Word of God and the testimonies stand or speak for themselves of the healing power of Jesus Christ. These people will never be the same. Those who have known these folks before ministry and after, their comments are all the same. They are amazed at the healing and the changes for the good. The things I have shared have come from my own experiences with brokenness.

There may be counsellors, therapists, and those in the psychiatric field who would question what I am sharing. I do not have the degrees or experiences that they have in this field. What I do have is God as my Lord and Saviour and His Word. I have the Holy Spirit who gives me wisdom and counsel and brings comfort to those who need healing. I also have God the Father who comes to comfort those who need to truly know the Father's Love.

There is nothing concealed that will not be disclosed, or hidden that will not be made known. What you have said in the dark will be heard in the daylight, and what you have whispered in the ear in the inner rooms will be proclaimed from the roofs.
Luke 12:2-3 (NIV)

To the Jews who had believed him, Jesus said, "If you hold to my teaching, you are really my disciples. Then you will know the truth, and the truth will set you free."
John 8:31-32 (NIV)

I seek God for His Wisdom in the ministry and as I humble myself, I trust and believe that He will guide me and show me my role, seeing that He always does His. (James 1:5) God is bringing much fruit to the ministry.

Meditation and Our Mind

God's Word tells us not to walk in the guidance of the wicked, or live like sinners, and those who enjoy mocking. If our desire is to meditate on the Lord and His Word daily, then we will be like a tree that is firmly planted by streams of water. God promises us we will bear fruit in season, and whatever we do we will be successful. (Psalm 1:1-3) We keep our way pure by living according to God's Word. If we hide God's Word in our hearts, it will help us not to sin. (Psalm 119:11) We must not neglect the Word of God. By staying in the Word of God, we will become wiser than our enemies. God's Word will give us more insight than any teacher around us.

God's Word will give us more understanding than anyone who is considered wise in the eyes of the world. God tells us in 2 Timothy 1:7 that He has given us the spirit of power, love, and a sound mind. The way to walk in holiness and purity is to be transformed by the renewing of our minds according to the Word of God. If we are renewing our minds daily, God's Word tells us we will be able to test and approve what His good, pleasing and perfect will is. (Romans 12:2) When we are grounded in the Word of God, the trials and sorrows of this world will not take us out. God's Word tells us He will never leave us and never forsake us. (Hebrews 13:5)

If we choose to meditate on and agree with the Word of God, then we can go from strength to strength and glory to glory. (2 Corinthians 3:18) As such, the human mind is very powerful and is much more dominant if we choose to keep our hearts and minds focused on God and His Word.

The person who does not know God does not accept the Word of God. God's Word is foolishness to that person because it is spiritually discerned. But God's Word says that the man who keeps his focus on Him, makes judgements about everything, but he himself is not subject to any man's judgement. As children of God, we have the mind of Christ if we stay in His presence and in His Word. (1 Corinthians 2:14-16)

If you have any encouragement from being united with Christ, if any comfort from his love, if any fellowship with the Spirit, if any tenderness and compassion, then make my joy complete by being like-minded, having the same love, being one in spirit and purpose. Do nothing out of selfish ambition or vain conceit, but in humility consider others better than yourselves. Each of you should look not only to your own interests, but also to the interests of others. Your attitude should be the same as that of Christ Jesus: Philippians 2:1-5 (NIV)

The Book of James talks about our trials and temptations. God tells us to consider it pure joy when we have to face such things. When we undergo these experiences, our faith is tested. Our trials and temptations help us to grow in perseverance and we become mature and complete, not lacking anything.

If we allow our meditation to be on the Word of God and desire His presence, then we can come to healing and wholeness. As we meditate on God's Word, our minds are renewed and our physical brain can be healed. Agreeing with and obeying the Word of God will change our thought patterns. He knows what prisons, pits, and dungeons the parts of our souls are trapped in, and He oversees the proper process of our healing. We can, as an act of our will, call back parts that we gave away to lies and things that were not of God. The heart that is fixed on Jesus will be kept in perfect peace. (Isaiah 26:3) God opposes us if we are proud, but if we will humble ourselves, He will pour out His grace on us. (James 4:6, 1 Peter 5:5) We must submit to God and resist the devil. (James 4:6-7) If we allow Jesus into our brokenness and into the dark places of our soul, He will heal us. Jesus is the Way, the Truth, and the Life. (John 14:6) As we invite Him into our darkness, He will bring us out of our captivity and into His love, joy, and freedom like we have never known.

"For who has known the mind of the Lord that he may instruct him?" But we have the mind of Christ.

1 Corinthians 2:16 (NIV)

God does not want us to walk in deception, but rather to put off our old ways of living in sin and to be made new in the attitudes of our hearts and minds. He tells us that we were once alienated from Him and were enemies in our hearts and minds because of our sinfulness. But now, as His children, we are reconciled to the Father by Christ's body through His physical death. As God's chosen, holy people and dearly loved, His Word tells us to clothe ourselves with compassion, kindness, gentleness, and patience. Forgive one another just as Jesus forgives us. The most important virtue on our part is to put on love, which binds these virtues in perfect unity.

God's Word directs us to prepare our minds for action, to be self-controlled, and to set our hope fully on the grace to be given to us when Jesus Christ is revealed. God desires the Body of Christ to love as brothers, being ready in heart and mind to walk in compassion and humility. God does not want us to repay evil for evil or insult for insult, but rather bless those who curse us. (Romans 12: 14-21) We can ask God to help us endure and give us a spirit of unity among ourselves as we choose to follow Him. Our aim as children of God is for perfection or maturity. Loving one another as we love ourselves will help us to be united in one heart, one mind, and one judgement. His desire is that we would live in harmony with one another, thus bringing glory to God. The Word of God calls us to agree with one another and in that way, we avoid divisions among ourselves.

If the call of the church is to walk in unity with one heart and mind, how can this come to pass if we are double-minded?

The only way to find peace is to be willing to release all control to Jesus and trust Him moment by moment, day by day. God encourages us to come to Him if we are weary and heavily burdened. He promises to give us the rest we need. Jesus tells us He is gentle and humble in heart and that we will find rest for our souls in Him. Jesus tells us His peace has been given to us and that we are not to be like the world focusing on our problems, but rather fix our eyes on Him, the author and perfecter of our faith. (Hebrews 12:2) God's Word also tells us to be still and know He is God. (Psalm 46:10) If we will still our hearts and trust Him implicitly, we will walk in peace. This peace is the kind that comes from Jesus. Let us allow the peace of Jesus to rule our hearts and be thankful in all circumstances.

God's Word tells us He will instruct us, teach us which path to take, counsel us and always watch over us. (Psalm 32:8) God also tells us if we will delight in the Lord by being soft and pliable in His hands, He will give us the desires of our hearts. (Psalm 37:4)

What a promise Jesus gives us! Let us choose to trust Jesus while waiting patiently for Him, remaining strong, taking heart, and being of good courage. All we ever require is there for the asking. Jesus is willing and able to help us and provide for every kind of need or situation we will ever face.

Therefore, as God's chosen people, holy and dearly loved, clothe yourselves with compassion, kindness, humility, gentleness and patience. Colossians 3: 12 (NIV)

*"The L*ORD *bless you and keep you; the L*ORD *make his face shine upon you and be gracious to you; the L*ORD *turn his face toward you and give you peace."* Numbers 6:24-26 (NIV)

Hope for the Shattered Scriptures

Behold, thou desirest truth in the inward parts: and in the hidden part thou shalt make me to know wisdom.
Psalm 51:6 (KJV)

But this is a people plundered and looted, all of them trapped in pits or hidden away in prisons. They have become plunder, with no one to rescue them; they have been made loot, with no one to say, "Send them back."   *Isaiah 42:22 (NIV)*

But this is a people robbed and spoiled; they are all of them snared in holes, and they are hid in prison houses: they are for a prey, and none delivereth; for a spoil, and none saith, Restore.   *Isaiah 42:22 (KJV)*

Hebrew meaning for robbed: to spoil, to catch, take for prey away, spoil utterly.

Hebrew meaning for spoiled: destroy, spoil.

Hebrew for holes: the cell of a prison, a hole, a cave.

Hebrew for houses: A dungeon, a prison.

Hebrew meaning for restore: rescue, return, recover, refresh.

Hebrew meaning for people: can be associated by implication to overshadow, hiding together as a congregated unit, a tribe, troops, or attendance, folk, a nation.

The Spirit of the Lord GOD is upon me; because the LORD hath anointed me to preach good tidings unto the meek; he hath sent me to bind up the brokenhearted, to proclaim liberty to the captives, and the opening of the prison to them that are bound; To proclaim the acceptable year of the LORD, and the day of vengeance of our God; to comfort all that mourn; To appoint unto them that mourn in Zion, to give unto them beauty for ashes, the oil of joy for mourning, the garment of praise for the spirit of heaviness; that they might be called trees of righteousness, the planting of the LORD, that he might be glorified. Isaiah 61:1-3 (KJV)

Hebrew meaning for broken-hearted: breakdown, broken in pieces.

Hebrew meaning for captives: exiled, take away, to transport.

Likewise, thou son of man, set thy face against the daughters of thy people, which prophesy out of their own heart; and prophesy thou against them, And say, Thus saith the Lord GOD; Woe to the women that sew pillows to all armholes, and make kerchiefs upon the head of every stature to hunt souls! Will ye hunt the souls of my people, and will ye save the souls alive that come unto you? And will ye pollute me among my people for handfuls of barley and for pieces of bread, to slay the souls that should not die, and to save the souls alive that should not live, by your lying to my people that hear your lies? Wherefore thus saith the Lord GOD; Behold, I am against your pillows, wherewith ye there hunt the souls to make them fly, and I will tear them from your arms, and will let the souls go, even the souls that ye hunt to make them fly. Your kerchiefs also will I tear, and deliver my people out of your hand, and they shall be no more in your hand to be hunted; and ye shall know that I am the LORD. Because with lies ye have made the heart of the righteous sad, whom I have not made sad; and strengthened the hands of the wicked, that he should not return from his wicked way, by promising him life: Therefore ye shall see no more vanity, nor divine divinations: for I will deliver my people out of your hand: and ye shall know that I am the LORD.   Ezekiel 13:17-23 (KJV)

Hebrew meaning for arm holes: hand of power, consecrate, forced parts, pain, terror.

Hebrew meaning for pillows: to cover sorcery, conceal (to fly), hide, overwhelm, full moon, festival, appointed time

Hebrew meaning for kerchiefs: to scatter, remove, consume, run, destroy, removal, smite

Hebrew meaning for fly: to break forth, to fly, make fly, to scatter, words, hum, chant.

Blessed are the poor in spirit, for theirs is the kingdom of heaven.   Matthew 5:3 (NIV)

Hebrew meaning for poor: to crouch, a beggar. Also, causing to fly away, to scare, frighten.

The eye is the lamp of the body. If your eyes are good, your whole body will be full of light. But if your eyes are bad, your whole body will be full of darkness. If then the light within you is darkness, how great is that darkness!
                                           Matthew 6:22-23 (NIV)

Greek meaning for "the eye be evil": hurtful, causing to fly away.

The Spirit of the Lord is upon me, because he hath anointed me to preach the gospel to the poor; he hath sent me to heal the brokenhearted, to preach deliverance to the captives, and recovering of sight to the blind, to set at liberty them that are bruised, To preach the acceptable year of the Lord.
                                             Luke 4:18 (KJV)

Greek meaning for broken-hearted: to crush completely - to shatter, break in pieces, broken to shivers, thoughts, mind broken.

If any of you lacks wisdom, he should ask God, who gives generously to all without finding fault, and it will be given to him.

But when he asks, he must believe and not doubt, because he who doubts is like a wave of the sea, blown and tossed by the wind. That man should not think he will receive anything from the Lord; James 1:5-7 (NIV)

We must understand that the trials we face in life are a door to the kingdom of God. Paul states in Acts 14:22, that it is through our trials that we enter the Kingdom of God.

The Greek meaning of "double-minded" means: two spirited or two-souled.

"Dipsuchos" is where we get our English word for schizophrenia, which is multiple personalities.

Dissociative identity disorder (DID) was previously known as multiple personality disorder (MPD). We may not necessarily have extreme psychological issues, but to be double-minded, or multiple-minded, is having one personality at home, one in the marriage, one as a parent, one at work, one at church, one with our friends, or one in difficult situations, etc. God tells us there is to be no shadow of turning. God wants to remove these veils, our double mindedness, so that we can see God with an unveiled face and be changed by His glory.

Testimonies from Brokenness to Wholeness

A bruised he will not break, and a smoldering wick he will not snuff out. In faithfulness he will bring forth justice
Isaiah 42:3 (NIV)

The names of those sharing their testimonies in their own words have been changed for their privacy.

The following testimonies speak for themselves.

My Own Journey

Some of what I have walked through in my life, I share in my testimony at the end of the book.

Growing up was very traumatic not only for me, but also for my twin brother and older sister. Our father and his parents were abusive to all of us. Every form of abuse began in the first year of my life, which caused physical, mental, emotional, and spiritual damage. Abuse also followed in two failed marriages. There are things that happened that I will not even put to pen. I will share my story of how many of my parts came up for healing and wholeness. I recall when our landlord's son stabbed me on the side of my head near my eye. I was a hair line away from losing my eye. I was only four years old. I clearly remember running down the lane as this troubled boy raised his hand to stab me, and how one part of me split off. Still today, I do not remember the actual stabbing.

During one of my healing sessions, I had a picture of me getting into bed with my father but nothing after that. I then saw myself in the arms of Jesus as He was taking me away to heal me. As I looked over His shoulder, I saw my pajamas on the bed. I quickly looked to see what I was wearing. Jesus had placed a soft white night gown on me. I asked Jesus "Why are my pajamas still on the bed?" He told me it was because they were defiled. He took me away for healing.

I used to spend my summer holidays at my auntie's country home by the beach in the Laurentians, Quebec. The man who lived next door to my auntie's country home was an awful person. One day he was over sitting outside visiting with my family. After we came in from the beach, we were instructed to rinse our feet off, go into the garage, remove our bathing suits behind a blanket, and hang them to dry. Then, with a wrapped towel around us, we were to go and get dressed in the house. As I passed by with my towel around me, the man from next door pulled my towel off me and I stood naked in front of everyone.

This abusive act traumatized me. It hurt me that my family did nothing about this. Everyone laughed at me. I was nine or ten years old when this happened. During the healing time for this event, I saw myself in the spirit, peeking out the front door of the house. I saw Jesus coming with a large, soft white blanket towards me. Jesus held it up high and looked away from me as He walked towards me. Even Jesus would not look upon my nakedness. He respected me and wrapped me in His soft blanket.

Jesus then took me to heaven. The white dress He put over my head covered me completely. After I let the towel fall to the ground, Jesus picked me up, carried me over to a tree and sat down. He cradled me in His arms, looked behind the tree and pulled out an old-fashioned divider, like the ones used in hospitals before they switched to curtains around the beds.

He pulled the divider around us so no one could see us and held me for a time of healing. As I watched this, I started to cry because Jesus cared about what had happened to me. Also, during this healing time I felt so loved, healed, and protected by Jesus. The core part of me was watching what was going on, as a part of my soul received healing. For most of my ministry times, the core part of me was able to watch the parts of my soul that came up for healing. The Holy Spirit showed me these things. I saw a picture of that part of my soul needed and receiving healing from Jesus.

Each human being has a spirit, a soul, and lives in a body. Because we are spirit, God can give us visions by the Spirit. There have been a couple of times during ministry that I had an actual open vision. That simply means I was seeing with my eyes open and everything in front of me disappeared. The Bible is full of stories of others having the same experiences.

I also had a part of me as a baby that would go to sleep during abusive times, allowing another part of me to move on with life. This part did not experience the abuse. During the ministry time I had a picture of myself sleeping and the part that split off could talk about this with no effects of the abuse. This is what the human mind/soul is capable of in order to survive trauma.

I also recall a part of me that came up and called itself the clown. This part was a twelve- or thirteen-year-old male. He said that when there was trouble in the home, he would start to joke and laugh, and it would change the negative atmosphere in the home. I knew I behaved this way at times but was not aware it was a part of me. This part came up for healing and wholeness.

During another ministry time I saw myself as a nun. I also saw a part of me naked, bruised, and dirty sitting in a dungeon. The nun was a split off from this part. During this ministry time with the nun, I saw Jesus come and start to remove her nun's habit. She was very nervous and held onto her cross around her neck. She prayed, asking Jesus to forgive her sins and be her Lord. Jesus put a beautiful wedding dress on her. Love, joy, and healing filled her heart. The minister at this time told the nun that the one sitting in the dungeon naked, dirty, and bruised was a split off from her. He asked her to go down and embrace this part and be one with her. I watched her go down into the dungeon, pick her up and saw her disappear into me, the nun. I asked that they come and be one with me. This ministry time brought great joy and peace to my heart.

Growing up in the Catholic religion sixty years ago, I do not recall any teaching about the love of Jesus Christ. There were many rules and much condemnation. I only saw God as someone with a beating stick and God help me if I sinned! I would spend more time wondering if my sin was a venial or a mortal sin. Hearing all this as a young person, together with all the abuse in my home, I was turned off religion and God.

There was also another wonderful ministry time with a part that was an Indian Chief. This split off was a very strong protector. The minister asked him if he was alone. The Chief told him he had a whole tribe to take care of. The minister asked him if he knew Jesus. He said, "No". The minister asked if he would like to meet Jesus and talk with him. The Chief said, "No. At that time, I saw a great big eagle coming toward me. The native people honour the eagle. This is one time when I had an open vision. The room disappeared and I saw an open range with mountains. It was all in colour. Coming over the mountain I saw a large eagle flying towards the Chief.

The minister asked the Chief if he would trust his life and his tribe to the eagle. He said, "Yes", prayed for forgiveness of sins and asked Jesus to be his Lord. He also called his tribe to come as well. When he prayed, I saw the Eagle open his great large wings and wrap them around the Chief and his tribe. They all fell under the power of the Holy Spirit. I watched the Eagle flying round and round, all the way up to heaven. I saw the Chief dressed in beautiful, white skin clothing that had beautiful beading on it. These parts received healing and became one with the core me. I will never forget this ministry time. My grandmother was half Native and French. This is probably why I chose to split off as a strong Indian Chief.

There was also another ministry time with a part of me who kept records of all that happened in our lives or in my parts. I saw her sitting at a table with other parts of me as well.

The minister asked her if she would come to Jesus and bring the others with her. She said she would like this but wondered what would happen with her books. She asked Jesus if she could bring them with her and He said "Yes." She prayed for the forgiveness of her sins and asked Jesus to come and be her Lord, and He healed all of them. Jesus came and brought all of them to heaven for healing. This part said Jesus was going to go through all her books and talk about them and bring healing to her and the others. I felt great peace with this ministry time.

During another ministry time I saw myself sitting in a courtroom and I was the judge. This part of me was very prideful and judgemental and passed judgement on anyone or any situation. The minister asked me if I would consider coming to Jesus. He told this part that Jesus is the Great Judge and paid for all sin and injustice. This took some time, but in the end this part stepped down and gave Jesus her robe and gavel. This part prayed forgiveness for all her sins and asked Jesus to be Lord of her life. This part was healed and became one with the core me.

During another ministry time, I saw a part of me wrapped in grave rags and covered in ashes. When I saw this part, I knew this part of me had died emotionally. This part of me was down in a prison cell. The minister saw two big angels with fire- faces come and bring me out of my prison. Jesus came and healed this part.

There are parts that do not integrate right away as they need deep healing. Jesus alone knows when parts are healed and ready to be integrated with the core person.

During another ministry time I saw a male part of me who looked like Mr. Clean - the one you see on TV commercials. He had large muscles and was in charge of many parts that were locked up in prison cells. He had a crowbar and if these parts cried, he would hit the bars and tell them to be quiet. The minister asked him if he would come to Jesus and give Him the keys to the cells so the little ones could come out, be healed, and set free.

He did not want to do this. God gave the minister a thought. He asked this part if Jesus could bring him a horse and what kind would he like. Right away I heard this part say, "Yes, I want a Palomino." I saw Jesus coming on a brown horse, bringing a beautiful Palomino. This part prayed for Jesus to forgive him his sins and be his Lord. He gave the keys to Jesus to go and rescue the little ones in their cells. I then saw him get on his horse and go racing with Jesus. I knew healing had come to all these parts. Jesus knows what will bring every part to Him. He is so amazing and loving.

I was watching the news one evening and heard about someone who had sexually abused children. I had thoughts while watching this, wishing this man would die. I asked God whether this was a part of me thinking this. God let me know that it was. I asked God what the name of this part was. He said, "Hitler." I was shocked and asked why would I call myself such a name? He told me to look at what was going on when I was young. I was born shortly after the 2nd World War. The world was coming through a terrible time of pain and sorrow and great abuse. Hitler had killed and abused so many Jews. God explained that because of the abuse I had suffered, I wanted to see any abuser suffer like the Jews did. I then saw a battlefield covered with dead soldiers. I saw Jesus coming to me with a soldier's helmet on. He picked me up and carried me over His shoulders. He placed me inside a Red Cross tent on a stretcher. He then closed the tent cover and said He was now going to heal this part of me.

During another ministry time a part that was angry and bitter came up for healing. This part told the minister that I had been shut down all my life. I was called the black sheep of the family. As a young child I was outspoken and told it like it was. I was angry and rebellious. I saw this part as a black sheep. The minister told this part, "Jesus wants to come to you and heal you." This part said, "Why would He come to me? I am so black." The minister told this black sheep, "We are all black and we can only become white sheep through the blood of Jesus." I then saw this little black sheep coming to Jesus with its head down, shaking, and full of fear. Jesus picked up the little black sheep and it turned white.

Jesus said, "I am healing you and you will never be mean or angry again." Jesus said, "I must hold this one for quite awhile for healing, as there is much pain and sorrow. This will take time." This little white sheep was still shaking in His arms. Jesus said the shaking would stop as He filled her with more of His love. Jesus said, "This one will grow quickly as the time is short." Jesus said, "I will do for her what she cannot do for herself. Jesus told the little white sheep, "Well done! You need to sleep and rest. You know you are safe in My arms." This little one said "Thank you" to Jesus for letting her talk.

There was another time when a friend of mine was ministering to me. She is also one of my intercessors during ministry times. She saw a doe and her little frightened fawns willing to come to Jesus. Jesus was waiting at a gate. As these little fawns passed the gate, they entered a beautiful, open green pasture. They knew they were safe. The next morning, I woke up and had the word fawns on my heart. I felt led to look up what a fawn was on my computer. A fawn is called a fawn for the first twelve months of its life. The sexual abuse began during the first twelve months of my life. I knew the doe was a part of me who protected the little fawns. I knew the fawn represented the first twelve months of my life. Many months later my friend emailed me a message that blessed my heart. In her own words:

"When I awoke this morning, I saw a picture of a doe, the protector, looking back into that place where all the little fawns had been imprisoned. I felt there were still some little fawns who had not dared to come out through the gate. Not a huge number, but they still needed to come out. The doe did not want to leave the vicinity of the gate until all were free. The little ones were feeble and scared to go alone. They came to Jesus, the Gatekeeper. He gave them food and stroked them with His hands. The Gatekeeper and the doe worked together to bring them to freedom and assure them they would be safe. Those who were free were willing to partner with the little ones who would come out.

"I told the little ones that Jesus the Shepherd knows where they are, sees their exact location and that He has always known where they are. I told those that were fearful, feeling useless and ashamed of their condition, that had been sheltered by the rocks, out of the light, just wanting to blend in and remain hidden, "The Shepherd sees and hears you. He never left in all this time, from the beginning of your life until now. He hears your weakest cry and is coming to get you, even those whose wool is so dirty that you blended into the granite rock cluster. He is *not ashamed of you.* He sees you through His eyes and is looking into your eyes. He is a Leader!! Look up, He is there. He hears your heart cry."

When I asked, "What would You do for this one?" He said, "This one is Mine." "He will carry and partner with you. You have such an important purpose and role in the days ahead.

You *will* make it! You will be the leader, the least of these!" All of them came and partnered with another one who was free.

The doe or protector was meek, grateful, and relieved that Jesus the Shepherd had never left. Looking back, the place is now very green, grassy and lush with wildflowers. It is a place of remembrance, but not bad memories. It can be visited.

Then there was another part of me that could be so, so angry. Whenever there was news of great injustice, this part would come up. One day I said to the Lord, "I am so tired of this anger. If healing could be today, let it be." I called a friend who would minister with me and told her how I was feeling. This angry part came up. In the spirit I saw what looked like a seven-year-old. I could feel this part hurting and angry all at the same time. I was crying, but it was really the emotions of this part.

My friend asked if Jesus could come and heal her. She did not respond. This part said, "I will not put up with this injustice." I saw Jesus standing in front of her. She told him she hated Him and that He did nothing to stop the abuse. She told Jesus He could have stopped it, but didn't. My friend asked this part to let Jesus know how she was feeling. I then saw this part start punching Jesus in the face and then she took hold of His beard with both hands and started shaking His head saying, "I hate you, I hate you." My friend said, "Let all your anger out. It must come out for you to have your healing." I then saw the seven-year-old with a knife in her hands, and she stabbed Jesus in His heart several times. Jesus lay on the ground and the seven-year-old started punching Him over and over and over. She finally fell over exhausted.

Then Jesus got up, picked her up, and held her close to His heart. After a while she had her head on His shoulder. I saw her lift up her head and spit in His face. She lay her head back down on His shoulder and cried again. Jesus said she had to let all the rage, anger, and murder she had in her heart go if she was going to be healed. Jesus said He would have to hold her for some time, as she needed much healing. Not long after this I could feel peace and healing coming into this part. I knew she had let go of all she had carried for many years. God is so good; He knows when we are ready to let go of the past and all the pain.

During this healing time I had been getting phone calls from my brother about some very hurtful things a member of our family was doing. When he would call and update me, I would feel such upset over the evil that was going on. Ever since this part of me came up for healing and wholeness, these phone calls no longer trigger me this way anymore. I am able to forgive and pray for salvation and healing and wholeness for this person. God does not say, "Do not be angry", but rather, "Do not sin in your anger." (Ephesians 4:26) We can hate the sin, but not the sinner.

I could share about so many other times of ministry, but feel this gives the reader an example of how Jesus comes to save, heal, and bring wholeness to the broken and shattered parts of the soul. There has been so much healing for my soul. I am experiencing more freedom from anger and fears. There is now a deep, deep peace in my heart and mind that I have never known. I am more gentle and calm. For the most part, things that would trigger me in the past have ceased. I have many comments from those who know me who say that they see the healing in my life. I have increased in my capacity to love and show kindness to those around me who are hurting. There is greater peace in my life overall.

I am not yet complete, but almost there. I have so much compassion for those who have suffered traumas, abuse, and neglect. I better understand why people behave the way they do. Broken people push others away, sometimes because of unreasonable demands or bad behaviour. This only causes others to avoid them. It's a two-way street. God has all the answers for our healing. I am hoping the testimonies will encourage and help others reading them to see their own need for healing. There is hope for all who would be willing to invite Jesus into their places of darkness and brokenness. Jesus loves every one of us. He longs to heal everyone, if they are willing to trust Him with their lives for wholeness.

Only Jesus can heal the broken parts of our souls. Splitting off comes as a result of abuse, trauma, and neglect. The enemy of our soul also comes to make sure we stay trapped in these places by putting us in some kind of prison, dungeon, or enclosure of our soul. The enemy can take the parts of our souls that are shattered and terrorized and trap us so we will not come to Jesus. This may sound strange to some reading about the shattered soul, but let the stories of many confirm this to be a reality. When my own healing first began, I really battled, wondering if this could be true about the human mind and what it can do. The folks who shared their testimonies for this book are strong, mature Christians who minister themselves. They are also folks who are well able to work, care for their families and prosper in many other ways. There are those who cannot hold down a job or have healthy relationships because they are so damaged. They need much love, patience, and time, in order to come to wholeness.

Our society has people in all walks of life who struggle with the same issues. It does not matter if you are a CEO of a company, in politics, a judge, a lawyer, a doctor, a pastor, a teacher, or a social worker. Many of us can suffer with brokenness. Many of us have triggers, parts that cause us to behave in ways that we cannot seem to change or stop. How often have you said, "Now why did I say that?" or "Why did I do this?" Although we can grow and change, there can still be times when we can just erupt or suddenly fall apart and have no idea why this never changes. It is usually an indication we are still trapped in issues of our past.

Because the heart and mind are well able to hide things from the past and keep them from the present, we become frustrated and confused about our behaviors at times. As I pray and minister, Jesus often shows me the parts. In order to minister to the shattered, I look for the wisdom and strategies of Jesus.

Only Jesus can heal the broken-hearted.

Brody's Journey

Hi my name is Brody.

Before I met Louise, I had little understanding about parts and soul fragments.
I was an on-fire, spirit-filled Christian, but my life was in shambles. Self-sabotage, anxiety, depression, self hatred, anger at God, and instability in every major life area were the norm. It was as though everything that I ever tried either failed or didn't work out, including making money or getting healthy. I would have moments of success ... lose the 50 lbs, win a contest, or get that new job. Yet, I would ultimately crash and burn. I didn't know it, but I hated myself and God got the blame for my failures.

I never attempted suicide, but I thought about leaving earth quite often. I wished the suffering would end and Father God would just take me home. I had lost all hope of being a success or living a consistent, happy, purposeful life. In my growing up years I was diagnosed with ADHD and other learning disorders. Maintaining mental and emotional health was always a struggle for me, and from the ages of 14 to 25, I was an alcoholic and a drug addict. Through it all, I was able to live a relatively normal life.

But, through Louise's ministry, I've been able to experience the greatest measure of wholeness that I have ever had in my adult life. This ministry has been a key component to my healing, wholeness, and life transformation. Through the process of bringing the parts of my soul back to Jesus and myself, which I will give you a glimpse into, the Holy Spirit has given me a greater understanding of the working of the human soul.

I wasn't sure if I had parts or not. I loved God, was born again, had healed the sick, prophesied regularly, and spent time with God. I was always in a huge battle to just feel "okay," never mind good. If I could just feel normal two days in a row, I would be ecstatic.

Then I met Louise!

I learned that throughout my life, my soul had split or created a part when I was unable to handle life as it came at me. Sometimes the splits happened because of traumatic events like drug addiction or childhood trauma, but sometimes it split even when I perceived something was too much to bear... even though it really wasn't that traumatic.

The first time I met with Louise, when we sat down, she prayed and asked if there were any parts of me that wanted to talk. She encouraged me to relax and just get out of the

way. As I relaxed into the couch, I was astonished when I heard a voice come up and speak.
"I'll talk," the part said. Louise proceeded to ask who this part of me was.
"I'm here to protect Brody."
"Protect him from whom?" Louise asked.
"From God."

I felt the toxic emotion of this part of my soul that was buried deep within, now surface. Louise started to share about God's goodness and that He is a loving Father. I was amazed how in that moment, what could only be described as a "false pleasure realm" was tangibly manifesting in my consciousness. It was comparable to the presence of God, but was a realm that I had created, to keep parts of me "feeling good" or safe. They would hang out there so I they wouldn't have to feel the pain of real life.

My eyes rolled and closed as this realm overtook me. Louise saw this immediately and persuaded this part of me that God's presence was better and real! It was amazing! This part of my soul became interested in God's realm and decided to come back to join Jesus and me. Louise led the prayer, and as I agreed and spoke it out loud, the false pleasure realm disappeared, and I saw that part go to join Jesus.

In that first session, this pattern repeated itself with other parts of me that had split off, and that had been wounded by my father. Seven parts were reintroduced to Jesus and me that day! Over the next weeks to come, I would work through multiple sessions with Louise over the phone where she would bring the good news of the love of God to any and every part of my soul that would listen.

After that first session, I felt so amazing the next week that I thought I was done! But, eight days later I started to have breakdowns again. I would get triggered by something and fall into a deep anger at God and then self-sabotage through binge eating fast food. I called Louise and we found that every time a trigger was activated, it was actually caused by a part of me that had split, and then manifested. It was as though a Holy Spirit inspired alarm clock let me know that there was another soul split to deal with.

Through the weeks I found parts of me that knew they were useless; parts that thought they were kings; parts that were left in pits of despair; parts that were in charge of many parts in armies of hundreds (these were parts that would escape into video games); parts that were playful, humorous and fun; parts that hated God; and parts that hated life. I even had a few parts that were female. As my father gave love to my sisters when I was young, parts of my soul split off thinking that if they could be female, they would be worthy of love. I had many parts that didn't even marry my wife and actually disliked her. This was interesting to learn and navigate.

It might sound ridiculous, but with each session, I would walk away with my life more intact, feeling more hopeful and better than ever. I learned that for people like me, the soul can split easily. If I didn't like something or had to face something painful, it was easier to just dissociate and forget, than to process the emotions and live life on life's terms.

Thousands of parts have now been integrated back into my soul with God, and I am living happier and more stable than I have ever been.

The biggest breakthrough came for me when, in a session, I saw a part of me that was in a prison. The prison was hope deferred. I have been given many large prophetic promises and my life was a complete contradiction to them. A large part of me split off and decided to live in the prison of hope deferred. Hope deferred makes the heart sick. (Proverbs 13:12) Since this part came to Jesus and me through Louise's guidance, my hatred of God has disappeared. How we view God is the most important thing in our lives. Our belief about God shapes our reality.

I'm very grateful to Louise for her unconditional love, guidance, and support in piecing my soul back together, literally.

Today I'm able to stick to healthy foods almost effortlessly, my connection and relationship with God has grown and developed in leaps and bounds, and I am learning to love my wife like God loves! I have business opportunities that came out of nowhere, and best of all, I am stable and whole, and when I look in the mirror, I actually like who I see. As a man thinketh in his heart so is he. (Proverbs 23:7) If your mind is divided against itself, it cannot stand. (James 1:8) Jesus is interested in healing and unifying every part of you with Himself.

I pray the shalom of heaven will be your portion, as you dive deeper into your spirit, whole soul, and body's union in Christ!

Kelly's Journey

I was raised in a Christian home and have been a Christian for over 19 years, with many victories in my years with God as my Lord. I believe in deep levels of healing, and I have experienced much healing in many different ways that God has used to set me free. I also believe that we have layers of hurts that God wants to heal us from, and He takes us through each one in its right time. As long as we are open to God, we can get through anything.

Along my journey I have found some recurring issues in my life and personhood that never seemed to be completely right. I struggled to feel confident in who I was; I struggled with acceptance and I also had a fear of rejection. One minute I would have confidence and strength in who I was, and then I would find I was doubting myself, suddenly convinced that I was not worthy of love or acceptance. This pattern affected me in every aspect of my life for many years with my relationships, my work, my friends, and my faith. I was struggling with conflicts within myself that would depress me at times.

When I was introduced to Louise and her ministry, I was skeptical. Not because I did not believe the ministry was good or real, but because I did not feel it was something I needed. I mentioned this to Louise and even while I spoke the words, I felt an inner desire to know more. When an opportunity came up a while later to meet with Louise, I jumped at the chance.

I quickly discovered this ministry was different than any I had ever experienced. I trusted God and Louise, and even though there were times it seemed uncomfortable, I stayed. I released the deep hurts and pains of my past to God. These were revealed as parts of me that had gotten stuck in the past. If for nothing else, just allowing these parts to be heard was a victory for me. I needed to know that it was ok that I hurt. It was ok for me to be angry and upset with the people and events that had hurt me, no matter how small or insignificant it seemed. I needed to know that God loved me even when I felt unlovable and unworthy.

I would like to share about some very significant parts out of the many healings that have made me whole through this ministry. These healings have changed who I am, how I am, how I think, and how I move. It is like I am a new person inside. Things I struggled with before no longer exist.

Casper

I mentioned that I struggled with rejection all my life. I experienced it and feared it so much that I would convince myself that everyone would reject me eventually. I was hurt and angry to the point that I put up barriers so no one could reach the inner me. But God knew the source. God helped me let my guard down and revealed the source of the rejection-the part of me that held my pain and rejection, the part of me that never grew up because of a traumatic moment when I was rejected by an older sibling at the age of three.

I love and admire my sister and always wanted to be with her. We were going out trick-or-treating and it was my first time. I was finally old enough to go trick-or-treating with my big sister and I couldn't wait. We started out together but soon I fell behind. I was too little and could not keep up. My sister was frustrated with me; she told me that she did not want me to follow her and that she did not want me there. She walked ahead and left me. That moment changed my life. I was rejected, I was deserted, I was not good enough, and I was alone. Casper, a separate part of me who never grew up, was formed, and kept me stuck in the past, at the very moment of trauma. I still had that three-year-old in me, convincing me I was not good enough. Fear of rejection set in at that early age and affected me throughout my life.

During the revealing of this part of me, I was encouraged to give the memory and pain to Jesus. I let him heal me of this moment and the effects it had over my life. I let Jesus take that part of me and bring wholeness. The child in me let go and gave the pain to Jesus. Immediately I was brought back to that very moment of my life in a vision, dressed up and alone in the street. Jesus came and He took my hand. My memory of that moment has changed, and I no longer feel the pain of rejection when I think of that day. All the emotions that came of that memory are gone and have been replaced with the new memory that Jesus gave me. That part of me has been healed and made whole again, no longer separate, and no longer controlling my emotions. Fear of rejection no longer controls me.

Order & Clutter

I struggled within myself throughout my life. One area of this was the desire to be organized and never achieving it. Even when my home was clean and orderly, I would struggle with the need for the space to be more organized. Most of the time I lived in a cluttered home because I would give up and I would feel overwhelmed. I would avoid my home if possible. I would shut down emotionally and become depressed if I had to face my mess. The strangest thing of all was that I was comfortable organizing and cleaning other people's homes, just not my own.

In one session with Louise, God gave her a vision of a neat, tidy woman, dressed like a banker. She started to describe the nature of this person and I soon realized it was the person I desired to be, but never seemed to be. God revealed that "Order" was a part of who I was. I longed to be whole in this area of my life, so I gave that part of me to Jesus and I was surprised to discover there were 2 parts attached to each other. "Order and Clutter" were twins or personalities that were opposite of each other, but very much a part of who I was. They could not be separated. One part craved order and another desired to be relaxed and messy.

These are two very different personality traits that are a part of who God made me to be. These parts fought each other daily in my life. It is ok to be orderly and it is ok to be messy. God healed me and showed me to love both parts of me. He showed me balance and how to become whole in these areas of my life. He took away the anxiety that was associated with the desire to be orderly and replaced it with peace. He gave me a new strength to face my clutter and not to feel overwhelmed when working to put my life and home in order.

At first, I did not notice the change in this area of my life until one day I had a strong desire to go home and work on cleaning my home office. I couldn't wait to tackle the piles of papers and boxes that I had ignored for many years. I didn't have the feeling of dread come over me when I thought of organizing my home. Instead, I felt peaceful and alive. I am no longer bothered by the mess and clutter of life while I work to stay organized. God has given me the ability to see past the mess and know that it is a work in progress, much like my life that God is still working on. It is freedom.

There is one significant moment in my past that changed my personality. Through prayer and trust, God revealed to me a moment when I was five years old and made a very serious decision that I had blocked from my memory until God brought it back. I was in kindergarten, and I could not tie my shoe laces properly. I was very shy and had little self-esteem. My teacher was frustrated with me because my laces were always untying. She yelled at me in front of all my classmates and that embarrassed me. I then hid in the fort of our classroom instead of playing with my friends. I felt like a fool. It made me mad, and at that moment I decided to stay mad and miserable. I decided to be unhappy. For whatever reason that I cannot understand, the child in me decided it was better to stay angry and unhappy than to let the moment go.

I never told anyone, and I blocked the moment out. I made a life and personality changing decision at that moment that stayed with me my entire life. I was no longer the happy child I once was. Instead, I was miserable, moody, and angry, always finding something to grumble about. I also had very few positive memories of my childhood because I chose to focus on the negative moments. Through this revealing, God showed me that my childhood was good, and that I had blinded myself from seeing good memories and enjoying them. I was stuck and needed to give God this moment and the vow I made. I asked God to forgive me and heal me of the embarrassing moment and all the losses I had because of my decision. He healed me and gave me flashes of many happy moments in my life that I had blocked out. Real moments of my past that are now part of my good memories instead of the negative memories. This part of me is now healed and whole within me.

Many parts have been revealed in my sessions with Louise. There are parts of me that define moments that represent disappointments and hurts I have experienced in my life along the way. And then there are the parts of me that have carried me through when I could not function on my own because the pain and disappointments were too much for me. Depression would set in, and I would shut down. But life goes on and I still had to get up each day and live my life. In one session it was revealed that these parts would carry me through the motions of each day. In a vision I saw myself lying in bed, in utter despair, pain and depression. These parts woke me up, got me dressed, fed me, got me where I needed to be, and helped me do what I needed to do. These parts were my strength, my guard, and my defender. There are no defining names for these parts, but these separate parts cared for me and kept life going when I could not get past a painful moment.

God wants us to be whole, not separated or fragmented. God is my strength, guard, and defender now. I don't have to rely on separate emotions and parts to get me through.

By giving these emotions, parts, pains, memories, disappointments, and dreams to God, I can now stand united as one. I only have to rely on my God. It is this God who heals me, makes me whole, strong, and the woman I am meant to be. God has touched the most intimate parts of me and made me whole. God has healed me. I am a changed woman because God loves me and met me in my most broken, most deeply hurt areas of my life and put me back together. I am no longer broken and shattered.

John's Journey

Here is my journey to healing through the process of *Hope for the Broken Soul Ministries.*

I wasn't sure if this was going to work or not, as I have been through an overabundance of inner healings and I entered into this healing process unsure of its effectiveness.

As I went to my first session, the Lord showed up in a unique way and started me on a healing process that no other inner healing session touched on, with the complete thoroughness that this healing process did.

As the Lord took me through some of my rough times, He was very quick to make sure that I didn't dwell on the negative aspects of what happened to me, by showing up in various modes of transport. Once it was a Harley motorcycle and another time it was a red Ferrari.

An amazing scene would play on the windshield, and I found myself back in the time where that trauma happened.

He was with me through to the end. Hundreds of little me's came together as one, as the forgiveness and healing process started. The Lord said that it would be a quick work and so far, it has been.

The result of this healing has been my ability to really trust people again and not have to put up all my defensive walls. The Lord is my older brother, and we are having quite a good time. I was never a gushy sort of guy with the Lord, and He is really quite ok with it, as he called me His younger bro.

It is really great to start to feel all together and this is what this healing ministry has helped me with. I look forward to more healing and wholeness as Jesus takes me through my journey into events of my past.

Cindy's Journey

I was raised in a Christian home and knew God early on, but struggled to know the depth of our Father's love for us. When I was about eleven years old, my parents got divorced. I was devastated because every kid wants their parents to be together. My mom and dad both had their own pain. When my parents got divorced, my mom made my dad out to be a bad person. Because of this misconception, my dad and I didn't end up seeing each other for a long time. Life was a constant struggle as I was always looking for that father's love and acceptance through other male relationships.

In order to fill the voids in my life and heart, I turned to other things. I started getting into the party scene and drinking a lot. I had a very hard life and experienced trauma after trauma. This trauma entangled me in the feelings of hopelessness, despair, and anger. I felt like I was in a constant circle that just kept going around and around and never changed.

As I grew older, the struggle still continued. I struggled to know my identity and I always felt like I was a little girl that never grew up. I longed to be set free and become the woman that God wanted me to be. The turning point in my life was when I met someone about five years ago. We ended up getting engaged. I thought I had found the love I've always wanted and needed. I was thrilled and excited. Yet it was actually an escape, a way out, a way to run away from all the pain, trauma, and bitterness I felt.

I recall telling one of my girlfriends that I was engaged, and I asked her to be part of the wedding. She was so gracious, but eventually she ended up telling me that the whole relationship wasn't right. I remember her saying that God spoke to her about me and said, "You need to tell her 'No'." When she told me this I didn't accept it and I was angry at her, but deep down I knew she was right. After praying about it, I knew I couldn't marry him. After I ended things with him, I felt like I hit my lowest point in my life.

I remember falling on my face before God and crying out to Him that I didn't understand. What's the point? I had nothing left. I said to God, "Take my life. Do what you want with it and whatever Your will, let it be done and make me into the woman you want me to be. Make me into a woman after Your own heart." After these prayers, God started to bring me through a season of healing. In this season, God took me through repentance and forgiveness. I was set free from a lot of strongholds that held me back in my walk with God.

One day the Lord spoke to me and said, "You need to make things right with your dad." So, after nineteen years, on Father's Day, I called up my dad and he answered the phone. We both cried and he said that he loved me so much. We ended up meeting up that day and I just remember his pulling up in his car. I couldn't wait for him to even get out of the car. I ran out the door of my place, and ran into his arms and wept. That day was not only a turning point for me, but it literally was like I was running into my heavenly Father's arms for the first time.

I was finally restored to my father, and it's like all the pieces of the puzzle were being put into place. Life has been like a whirlwind since then, and God has done so many great things for me! God restored my relationship with my father and his entire side of the family. I have a wonderful stepmom! My father got me a car and found me a place to live. He paid off all my debt and got me a new job! He also helped me get on the worship team at church and this brought me even more healing. After everything I had been through, I had a lot of parts that needed healing and wholeness. A few of the parts that really affected me most were the parts that were unable to trust.

These parts really affected my life and relationships with men. After God brought healing to those parts of me, I was not suspicious anymore or afraid to trust others. I also had a part of me that was unable to feel real. That part was terrible. I believe that I developed that part because of all the trauma that I went through, and that was my way of coping. Jesus healed that part! Praise God! I was about eight years old in the vision He gave me. As Jesus was healing me, I saw Him dancing and spinning with me, and He also did a puzzle with me. Since the healing of that part, I haven't had that feeling of not being real anymore. Also, a part of me always felt like I had to be perfect and to perform. I had to be perfect in everything that I did.

During another ministry time, I asked God to give me a new heart; I asked Him to heal my broken one. God gave me a vision: I was holding out my hands with all the broken pieces of my heart and Jesus took the pieces and started to tape them together. I was looking at my heart all taped together, and it started to turn into a new heart that wasn't broken anymore. You couldn't even make out the tape lines anymore. God picked up the new heart, and He put it in me. Then He reached in again to touch the heart, and it started beating.

I had a part that came up that was a strong protector. While God was healing me, He gave me a vision. We were at war, and He was standing in front of me. I crouched down, hidden behind Him. People were firing shots at Jesus and the Lord was taking all the shots. Jesus was taking the wounds for me. There was actually a point where He was getting shot so much that He started to bend over top of me. The Lord showed me that He is my Strong Protector.

As more parts were getting healed, Jesus gave me a vision where my family was starting to link together, and it started with Jesus. We all linked together and started to form a line whilst holding hands. Restoration is coming to my entire family.

Another part of me was being healed and the Lord gave me a vision where we were dancing together. I saw a vision of Him praying for me and interceding for me. Then I was standing on a hill and the Lord's hand reached down and pulled me up and started cradling me in His arms. As God was healing me from this part, He showed me a mirror and showed me how He saw me; he told me how beautiful I was.

This process of being healed from parts has been hard at times, but it's changed me for the better God has healed me much, more than I can ever imagine. I went from being broken and shattered to becoming a woman and finding my identity in Christ.

I want you to know that no matter what you have been through: the traumas, the pain or the anger, that the Lord is with you, and He is eager to heal you if you will allow Him into the past traumas of your life.

There is hope and He loves us all!

Be Blessed!

Sharon's Journey

I was conceived out of wedlock. My mother had run away from her first husband with my six-year-old sister. Promises of not drinking were made and broken to my mother, by her father and alcoholic brothers, causing her to run to my future father for reprieve and consolation.

While my mother was pregnant with me, my father was incarcerated for perjury before a judge. My mother gave birth to me alone, without my dad as he served his sentence in jail for almost two years. My father and his only brother endured a sad, harsh, and cruel mother and an alcoholic and henpecked father. Both my father and grandfather were extraordinary, respected businessmen, with no formal education other than correspondence. I am very proud of their courage. Despite this dynamic in my dad's home, I knew both my grandparents loved and enjoyed me, infrequent as our visits were.

Closet alcoholism and unfaithfulness were a cycle in my father's heritage. My grandmother had seduced my grandfather away from his first bride at age seventeen. My grandmother gave birth to my dad and his younger brother shortly after.

At around four years old, I broke out in head-to-toe festering eczema. My parents tried every doctor and source to find relief, and nothing helped. In a round aluminum tub placed on the kitchen floor, I would be routinely stripped and soaked in an oatmeal bath. I felt ashamed. My raw skin needed long cotton strips to cover them every day. I cried a lot and wanted to scratch even when there was no skin, only open sores. A part of me split off then because I had to endure, be strong, and be brave.

Oral Roberts, a faith healer and preacher, was coming to Calgary to have a tent crusade. We were going! That night after the message, I stood with my parents in a very long line, with hundreds of desperate people, to be personally prayed for. My turn came and I believed God could heal me. I went home and nothing extraordinary happened. BUT gradually all the eczema disappeared, leaving only one scar on each arm to remind me that God can do anything!

As a teen I was fortunate to be in a large youth group in our church. I now realize playing piano, singing duets, having lead roles in drama, plays, dating the best of the best, were all gifts given by God to show His love, but I had extremely deep parts of shame, fear, and worthlessness. I refused to believe I was worthy of any true love and favours.

I married and had three children. When a part would surface in a situation, I would ask my husband, "Is there something wrong with me?" He would always say, "No." That question nagged me.

When I began my journey to recognize the need for, and seek healing, I was a grandmother who had made many mistakes. How could I change and have new patterns? How I do I connect with a part —what is that, anyway?

The first part that came to Jesus was Shame. I saw Jesus standing and waiting to cover me. I cried because safety and peace had come at last! Worthlessness came to Jesus. I dreamt I was in a clear, square glass elevator that was going way down, down deeper than the building itself, going to a place where Jesus knew the deep roots of hidden experiences were kept. When I awoke, I felt so clean and free! All was clear in the elevator.

Abandonment and Rejection came to Jesus. I asked Him to forgive me for my sins and asked Him to touch me. That night I dreamt again. I saw a toddler maybe a year old, standing in a play pen in a pink one-piece fleece sleeper. My father entered the room wearing coveralls, work boots and gloves. He came directly over to me and smiled, looking directly at me, and left as if in the middle of a job. He saw me! He loved me! Such peace settled me down in a way I had not known before. Thank You, Lord!

Different parts of painful memories continued and still carry up to the surface as I am willing to be quiet and wait to see what the Holy Spirit brings to my memory, an impression, or words in my mind. Louise willingly gave of her time and listening heart, and she is extremely chosen by God to bring wounded and broken people to wholeness and completeness. She was another blessing to both my husband and me.

There is healing to all who would be willing to allow Jesus to come into the places of brokenness and trauma.

Blessings.

Mary's Journey

I once heard that when God is preparing us to come to earth, He gives us an idea of who our family will be, and what the journey of our life will be like on earth to become overcomers and spend eternity with Him.

I am not sure whether or not that is true, but I wonder how many of us would sign up for the journey we have been on. Fortunately, when we come to earth, we are not on our own.

The Lord sends angels to watch over us, and His Spirit is present with us to influence us for good and to get us going in the right direction.

Thank God, I seemed to have a double portion of the latter, being born into a family where both sets of grandparents were church-going people of faith, and God was the single greatest reality in my life. I had a sweet, loving mother for whom I will be forever grateful, and who was always there when I came home from a not-so-nice day at school. Her love and warmth will forever stand out as the constant balm to my soul during my formative years. She continually honoured the Lord, seeking God's will for her and her family.

I am sure her prayers kept me out of a lot of ditches, and have been the reason for many of the blessings in my life.

My father was a tall, strong, quiet man to whom I constantly looked to for more than he was able to communicate with me, in word and deed. My siblings consisted of an extremely wounded older sister, who made life difficult for me at times, and two younger brothers who were delightful. They were the main reason that when I got married, I thought that if I had a choice between all boys or all girls, I wanted all boys!

There were a lot of problems and sadness in my extended family, and plenty of folk outside my family, to help the enemy of my soul sow seeds of rejection and create a lot of brokenness in me. So, I was not spared from the wiles of the devil, who sowed seeds of insecurity and inferiority in my life at an early age. Since it was people that I looked to for love and acceptance, the devil used to do the most damage through people; I had a lot of rejection issues.

One of the hardest blows of my life was when my husband of twelve years told me he was in love with another woman, and thus divorced me on the grounds that my religion made cohabitation with me intolerable. The thing in life that was most important to me, my relationship with Jesus Christ, was intolerable to him.

Well, needless to say, I needed a lot of healing from all the slings and arrows life shot at me, but the Lord has been very gracious to me. The journey toward wholeness began almost as soon as I was baptized in the Holy Spirit in 1973. This was through different ministries who offered information on how to restore your soul, what the Bible refers to as "being transformed." It was a slow process, inch-by-inch I would say, until 2010.

Since then, I have been making leaps forward in the process. The first leap forward came when I discovered that insecurity and inferiority are the two things that the devil sows in everyone's heart to begin his destructive work in their lives. I was able to finally see the root of all the struggles in my life! I had a great release from these things in the core of my soul in 2010 after being in an anointed church service for a couple of hours.

After this breakthrough, I felt a lot better for the most part, but as time went on, I could sense there were still negative things manifesting in my soul at times that I should not be feeling about myself or others as a child of God. It was during this time that my dear friend and sister in the Lord, Louise Franck, began telling me about the ministry to parts, as she called them. Well, the first time one of these parts became clear to me was when I said to Louise, "I believe there is a part of me that is still longing to have my father play with me and give more input into my life."

So, Louise graciously asked me if I wanted her to pray for this part and I said, "Yes." When she began to address this broken part of my soul, I soon saw in my spirit a part of me that was about six years old, sitting with my knees drawn up to my chin, feeling sad and wanting my daddy. Louise asked this part of me if she would let Jesus come in and heal her. She resisted for a bit and then said, "Yes." I then saw Jesus come and lift her up on her feet. They hugged. While this was happening, my father came into the picture and for a moment I wanted to go with him, but Louise told me to stay with Jesus and He would heal my heart. So I did and Jesus did. And to this day I do not have the feeling that I need my father any more, but I am just thankful for the dear, good man who was there to father me the best he knew how, and set a wonderful example of honesty, integrity, and many other virtues which I admire and appreciate him for.

There have been many other parts, and I won't go into detail, but I will share a few of them. There was one who wanted to be a man, because of male strength and independence, compared to the vulnerable position I had been put in through the circumstances of life. Another wanted to be a tough girl who rode a motorcycle alongside the guys. I called her Bertha - ha! - so unlike my core personality, which obviously she saw as weak and vulnerable. The most recent healing of a part of me was a couple of weeks ago. This was probably the part that did the most crying of all of them. She called herself Nameless, because she felt she had no voice about the hurtful circumstances I had walked through in life. She was hurt and angry at everything and everyone who had caused pain.

Including being angry at me for marrying my ex-husband, leaving my parents in the U.S. and coming to Canada. And Canada! This is where the worst of my pain happened.

Well, bless the Lord, because to my knowledge, Nameless is healed. Since this last part was healed, I have the greatest peace that I have felt in my life.

My heart is open to any further healing that the Lord wants to do in my heart and soul. I want to be completely whole.

When Jesus walked the earth, He said to someone, "Be made whole!" And they were made whole. I hope that my testimony will encourage you to believe that you can be whole as well, and let Jesus heal every broken part of you!

Blessings.

Anna's Journey

Like many of you, I have experienced trauma and wounding in my life. I believe that even in the womb I experienced rejection. Rejection has been a huge issue in my life!

It had a way of showing up, re-wounding me because I agreed with it. I would tell myself, "Obviously I am not the kind of person people want or like to be around." I was shy, introverted, and insecure. In time, bitterness and self-pity joined rejection in its line-up.

As I matured into young adulthood, I became more confident and sure of myself. But, when rejection would come along in any form, I would spin out like the childhood spinner tops we played with. I was triggered, and what showed up and acted out was not nice to behold. I would be tormented and confused.

I could almost see myself becoming this other person.

But I didn't understand for years what this was.

I met Louise in 1995. She was a new Christian, and I had been one for 35 years. But what grabbed my attention were her passion and her boldness regarding the things of God and His ways. I might add that it was so different from the way I was raised and taught in my church. It has not surprised me at all that God has directed Louise into this journey of healing of the soul. She has been a willing vessel in God's hands as He has taught her about parts. She was open to all that God has for her. I on the other hand, came along cautiously and skeptically.

That is, until Louise started to minister to me! Then these parts showed up, cautious and skeptical too.

I had been in bondage too long and had suffered too much pain by these unpredictable parts showing up and acting out. I was ready to participate fully in this healing ministry.

We are all unique and respond uniquely in this ministry. There is no right or wrong way. I just go with it.

I learned that closing my eyes helped me visualize as Louise ministered to me. At first, I tried to analyze and figure out what was going on. This halted the process completely. I let that go, and just reported what I saw; God and Louise did the rest. These parts came forward for healing through repentance and coming to Christ. Then each part was integrated into my soul to become one with me.

At times I experienced a change fairly quickly. At other times it was more like, "Wow! When rejection was triggered, I did not react in my old ways." Or, looking back on the incident, I recognized that I did not spin out like I used to. Healing was in process.

Freedom, indeed. Inner healing, indeed. Brokenness becoming whole.

I would like to share with you a particular session. After addressing the part and praying, Louise would ask, "Is Jesus coming to you? What does He look like?"

In this instance, He arrived sitting on a burro and wearing a sombrero. He was twirling a rope in the air, "Chill out, girls!"

I was always very serious because life has been hard! But when He arrived in such an efficient, yet relaxed manner, I had to laugh. He had it all under control!

This happened another time when I was quiet in God's presence after I asked Him to speak into my life. I was sitting alone in a pit with ashes. I looked up and saw Jesus coming towards me. He was laughing, carrying a stick with a wiener on it. He sat down across from me and continued laughing and chatting up a storm! I was no longer alone. He showed me that He wanted to be with me. I just could not get over it. Jesus loved being with me. Period! I did not have to look good, be good, or try to up my approval rating.

I do not get a picture every time. Sometimes I get a single word, or a scripture verse or a phrase. Sometimes I go into a Bible story and Jesus is there to give me understanding as to how this story is relevant to me.

Oh, it is so comforting that He meets us where we are and knows exactly what our pressing need is. He also knows when we are ready.

Sometimes He ministers to us through others like Louise. No judgement, no condemnation, just compassion and love. Sometimes He shows up by the Holy Spirit's leading and facilitates the encounter.

How good our Father is to us. How much He desires to set us free, to heal us, to make us whole.

I am forever grateful to God for bringing Louise into my life. I have been so blessed because she has been obedient to the leading of the Holy Spirit in her life. She is a spiritual warrior, a woman of great courage and inner strength who loves the Lord her God with all her heart, with all her soul, and with all her mind. (Matthew 22:37)

My prayer for you is that you too will receive healing and wholeness in the broken parts of your soul.

In Jesus' Name

Amen.

Betsie's Journey

One evening Louise and I were waiting for a friend to arrive for ministry. I was there to pray and record while Louise ministered to the individual. While we were waiting, Louise said to me, "Betsie, do you think some of your parts would like to come up and be one with you?" Five little blonde-haired girls immediately showed up in the spirit. They were standing around me, smiling and were four to seven years old.

Louise asked them if they had Jesus in their hearts and they quickly responded, "Yes." Louise asked them if they would like to one with Betsie. They responded, "Yes." Louise led them in a prayer to be one with me.

I believe these little girls were split-offs or parts as a result of the trauma they experienced as young children. My Dad was a WW1 vet whose brother's head was shot off when they were running in the trenches in Belgium in 1915. He was sent home with what we now call PTSD. He would drink and become angry and abusive to my mom. I grew to hate and fear him. I would even pray that God would kill him or stop him from coming home.

Another trauma in my young life was when my twenty-five-year-old brother-in-law molested me when I was five years old. I never told anyone about this.

After Louise prayed for these little girls to be integrated with me, I felt a greater degree of joy and peace.

I had already forgiven my dad and brother-in-law for these offences, but now I do not even think about these things anymore.

Before my dad died, he asked God to forgive him, and he gave his life to Jesus. I look forward to being with him in heaven.

God is good.

Veronica's Journey

When I was 12, I was at a sleepover with a friend where we played a "game" of touching each others' bodies. I returned to school and told my schoolmate, who told everyone in my class. I was called names, ignored, rejected, and isolated by my whole class. This broke my spirit and caused great shame and guilt. I didn't speak about it for many years. When I asked Louise to pray for me, she was able to lead the 12-year-old part of me through a process of asking Jesus into that situation, and Jesus reconnected that 12-year-old part of my soul with me as an adult. I was no longer stuck in past trauma. I felt such relief! My spirit felt full! The shame and guilt were gone! I was set free. Now, I feel such incredible light and wholeness in my body. I am at peace and no longer tormented by those memories and feelings. I did not know that I had grown so numb to spiritual things, but now I can sense God's presence and feel God so close to me. It is like I had been asleep and now I am awake. What an incredible blessing and gift.

God healed me of poor stewardship and poor financial management. When I was little, I always spent all of my allowance, and when I was older, I spent my pay checks as soon as I received them. God showed me that this was generational, and that I did not have to live under this anymore. He showed me that I was covered with clay in my spirit – like a mud mask – and He was shaking me so that all the clay was cracking and shaking off. I am healed and I am whole. I have such great hope for the future.

This picture describes parts of the soul still trapped in traumas of the past.

The Prayer

And now as you have read our stories, lets pray.
I seek for the Holy Spirit to be upon me as I pray these words: Thank You Jesus for Your guidance and presence along the way of my life's journey. I pray and ask to live wisely, allowing the peace of Christ to rule in my heart. As your Word says, "I love those who love Me, and those who seek Me find Me." May I truly understand Your passionate love for me, Lord, as I seek and find You. I ask now for Your Almighty strength to forgive those who trespass against me so I may release my burdens. I no longer accept the pain and suffering, the trauma and anger. I release all of it to You now, oh Lord God. I ask forgiveness of my own sins that have come between us. I accept all You have given in this time of healing and forgiveness that I may love deeper than I ever imagined possible. I ask You for peace and hope for those who have wronged me. I ask for love and hope for my own heart to be healed in Jesus Name. As Christ gave His life, I surrender to You now, Jesus Christ. I ask, Jesus, that You bring the right partnerships to me that would allow my relationship to grow with You and for You. Amen.

Written by Lana Saretsky

My Life before Jesus Christ

I was born and raised in Rosemont, in the east end of Montreal, Quebec. I was part of a family of five: my mother and father, older sister, my twin brother, and me. My brother and I were born in 1947, not long after the Second World War, when times were still difficult for many people. We lived in a one bedroom upstairs flat. My parents slept in the living room, and only a curtain separated us from their bedroom. My twin and I slept in the same crib until we were around two years old. My sister slept in a bed beside us.

My sister didn't know our father for the first two years of her life, as he was in the army reserve in Jamaica. When he returned, he expected her to jump into his arms and show affection toward him. He disciplined her from the day he returned. That only caused her to be afraid of him throughout his life and she was never close to him.

When my mother was pregnant with my twin brother and me, there was only sickness for all of us. We were born two months premature, and all three of us were dying. We were given the last rights by a bishop. By the grace of God, we all lived.

Life was difficult for our mother from day one, as my father's parents never accepted our mother, who was Protestant. Coming from Quebec, she was marrying into a Catholic French family. That was not a good start. Today we know there are still issues between French and English and between those who are Protestant and Catholic.

My father was raised by very abusive parents and in turn, he abused our mother and us. There was every form of abuse: mental, emotional, sexual, and spiritual abuse. Our grandparents, as well as our father, were involved in great darkness. The first six years of our lives were also filled with abuse from our landlord and his son. The son would put broken razor blades in our hands so that our hands would drip blood. He would spit on us. One day, he scratched my sister's face from top to bottom with his fingernails. Her face was covered with blood. The son would also hide under the long staircase in the back of our home and pull our legs out from under us. We would then go flying down the stairs and land on the concrete in the back lane. This landlord's son was constantly hurting us. The father was verbally and physically abusive towards his son. He would also spit at his son and encourage him to do the same things to us as little children. No wonder his son was full of violence. One day, this son chased me down the lane with a pocketknife and stabbed me by the side of my eye. The family doctor said I was a hairline from losing my eye. At this point, my mother took the landlord and his son to court. The courts sent the son to a boys' farm for troubled children. We moved to an apartment building when I turned six. While we lived there, a couple of men who lived in the same building also abused me.

My grandparents and father were involved in the occult. I recall that any time I entered their home I could literally feel hands touching me. My grandmother was very cruel to our mother and that is a story in itself. My grandmother gave my parents a stove when they married. One day she came over to their home and sold it to someone. She told my mother, "I bought it and I can do what I please with it." She would hit my mother and slap her face if she was upset over the smallest issue.

Our father and his parents found great pleasure in being cruel, traumatizing our whole family. My grandmother had such a violent temper that she almost killed our father with an iron rod from the wood stove. A neighbor saw this and ran over to rescue him and pull my grandmother off of my father My grandmother also played my father and his younger brother against one another. She would lie about what one said about the other to keep them apart. She would also use money as a tool to control them. That's what I know of his early life and then, for all of his adult life, our father was involved in multiple affairs. This went on until he died. My father grew up watching his own parents becoming involved in many affairs. Life was one of constant fear, arguments, and much abuse. I lived in fear every time my grandparents would babysit me or when my father would come to my room He would take separate holidays in the summer at my aunt's log home. My father would have me sleep with him. I have some memory of getting into bed but no memory of what happened. Jesus took me back to heal me but did not allow me to experience the trauma all over again. God is good.

I know my sister and twin brother also suffered fear, trauma, and abuse from our father and his parents. My brother has little to no memory of his childhood days. That is what happens when life is so traumatic. I know the human brain is very capable of shutting out what a person cannot bear and finding a way to go on.

The abuse never stopped. After years of this, fear and anger grew inside of me. It was hard to focus on classroom time. It was all I could do to have passing grades. I could only maintain average marks. My life from the start until I left home was filled with every kind of abuse. During the first five years of school I was able to achieve honours, but after that my marks went down to average marks. I could no longer focus in the classroom. I would lose class time worrying more about what would happen when I got home.

I saw my mother crying a lot as our father would argue with her for hours. He would exhaust the whole family. I also could not bring friends home, as my father was inappropriate with one of my school friends. He would make promises to us and break them with a smile, but he was also violent with us and made embarrassing public scenes. When we went to church the odd time, he would sing so loud everyone would turn and look at him. My father would speak so loud in public when angry that everyone would hear him. By the time I was fifteen, I was full of fear, anger, and rage.

Our father had what we call a champagne taste and a beer budget. All through my parents' marriage, my mother worked hard to keep up with my father's debts. Our mother's family, including us kids, helped our mother out with paying off his debt. My father hurt his back and had to be hospitalized. While he was in the hospital, the doctors told my mother he was a psychopath. One doctor said, "You have a very, very sick husband."

There is so much I could write about, but I believe this is enough to say life growing up was traumatic.

Our mother lost her health in her thirties. She had many health problems and surgeries until she died at fifty-four of cancer. We spent most of our young years, until we ourselves were married, visiting our mother in the hospital. One time, after her first cancer surgery, my father's first question for the doctor was not "How is she?" or "Does she have cancer?" but "Can she still have sex?" Years later, during the last few hours of my mother's life, the only thing our father could talk about was what kind of tombstone he should buy for her. My brother took my father by both arms and escorted him out of the room. My father left the hospital and did not return.

The next day, we told him our mother had passed away. My

parents had been separated for one year, so she had a separate bank account. When she passed away, the first place he went was to her bank to see if he could access her account. Even today, I do not know how he managed to access it, but he did.

I met a man when I was eighteen and married him at twenty years of age. I loved him very much and I was happy to leave home. What can I say? The one thing I longed for was to be loved, honoured, and respected. Not knowing what that looked like, I ended up marrying a man who was broken himself. He was born out of wedlock and never knew his own father. He was abused by a stepfather. His mother died of cancer in her forties. He then went to live with his uncle who was abusive, and then during his teenage years he was raped by an older man. It seems that broken people marry broken people. If you have never known what real love or honour or respect looks like, you just make choices by what you have experienced.

After we were married for a year, I became pregnant. That is when the abuse started in our marriage. He was very angry that we were going to have a child. He was also a man who ran up debt without letting me know. The I found out when the loan officer called me to say he was behind on his payment. In the middle of the night, he would kick me out of bed while I was in a sound sleep. He told me after we were married and had our first child that he never loved me. He said he knew I could make a good wife because I could cook and clean for him. He was also rough with our son at eighteen months old, so I forbade my husband to ever touch him again. We had a daughter four years later and a son eighteen months after that. By this time, I was already brokenhearted in my marriage. I was determined to be such a good wife—surely he would love me then.

Our son Andrew was very ill for the first twelve months of his life. I spent many hours with him in the ER for ear and throat infections. By the time he was twelve months old, he needed his tonsils and adenoids removed. By the time our son was four, he was already showing feelings of anger. He knew his father did not love him.

When Andrew was four years old, I gave birth to my daughter Linda. This was a wonderful time but also a difficult time. My mother died two weeks after my daughter's birth, but she was able to see our daughter and to know that I had named Linda after her.

Eighteen months later, I became pregnant with twins but lost one of the babies in the first trimester. The surviving twin, James, was born with many medical problems. At birth, he was taken to the ICU as he was blue and had difficulty breathing. A few days later they brought him to me. He was doing well, but I noticed his head was an odd shape. At his six-week checkup, the doctor told me he required surgery. His skull was closed and was not allowing the brain room to grow. He also had double pneumonia, a heart murmur, and a twisted foot. In order to have two surgeries on his skull, he was placed on the seventh floor ICU for a few months. At the same time, my son Andrew was on the fourth floor with spinal meningitis. I spent time going between both floors caring for them, not knowing if they would live.

When James was fifteen months old, my friend was babysitting him, and her elderly uncle left his medications out. James ate them all and was rushed to hospital. Shortly after I arrived, he went into a coma. He was in ICU again. The doctors could not say if he would recover. When a doctor tells you so many times that they do not know if your child will make it, you know it can only be God when he does recover. I always believed in the one true God and Jesus Christ but did not have an understanding of salvation. If you knew how sick my sons were, you would say, "Only God." By the grace of God alone, he came through all of this with no side effects.

My son, Andrew, also came through meningitis with no side effects, but then six months later, Andrew came down with another form of meningitis. Again, he recovered with no side effects. The doctors were so amazed at his recovery.

During these years my daughter, Linda, did not receive the attention she needed. I was able to feed and clothe her and spend minimal time with her. I spent most of my time with her sick brothers. During the time my son James and his older brother were in hospital, their father came once to see Andrew, but never to see James. That was enough for me. After my children were "out of the woods" and healthier, I considered this the best time to leave the marriage.

I thank God for my sister Maureen who helped care for Linda during this trying time. Once, I happened to stop by to see my aunt and uncle who lived near the hospital to update them on my boys, and my father showed up while I was there. I continued to keep him away from my life till he died. He was never a safe person to be with. He never came to see any of the children in their illnesses or difficult times. The only thing he could say to me was, "Let me know if they die, and I'll come to the funeral."

During the last year of my marriage, I met someone and fell into adultery myself. Even if my marriage was over, I still had no right to allow this to happen. This ended in heartache as well.

I finally left my husband after ten years of marriage I received financial aid from him for only a few months. About forty years have passed since that time and the children have never heard from him.

About three years later, I met someone I fell in love with. I moved out of town with him and had a surgery that allowed me to give birth to my fourth son, John. I was unable to work during my pregnancy. I was not strong at the time, as I had major surgery in order to conceive. The surgery meant that I would be recovering for some time and that carrying the child would be painful and difficult. At this time, I needed John's father to help financially for our food and basic needs, but he ignored my request. It was then that I made friends with some wonderful neighbors. One of these ladies paid me to clean her home which helped with groceries.

I soon learned many things about my second husband. His own childhood had been filled with abuse, what could I have expected? We married when our son was eighteen months old. I so wanted this marriage to work. It did not take long to know that he did not care for me or my children from my previous marriage. Our son from this marriage was also born with health problems. When he was six months old, he only weighed eleven pounds. We were referred to a specialist who diagnosed him with cystic fibrosis He was put on daily treatments of oxygen several times a day. My local family doctor did not believe John had cystic fibrosis and put John on a special milk formula and we watched him prosper after this change.

I realized at this time that I had married a man whose greatest love was money. He did not feel accepted by his family. He once took a picture of the house he had built, with his expensive car in front of the house, and sent the photo to his family. He felt that if they saw his possessions, it would compensate for never having gone to university as so many of his family members had. Money made him feel acceptable and was more important than anyone in his life.

At seven, my son John went to a Christian Bible Summer Camp for a week with some good friends of ours. At this time, John decided to trust Jesus Christ with his life. He returned home and asked me to have him baptized. We looked for a church, and he was baptized.

Not long after this, my husband came home from working out of town only to tell me my son Andrew had an accident. By this time my son was in his early twenties and had left home. He worked out of town with his stepfather.

The truck he was driving had slid on ice and hit a propane tank. When the tank burst into flames, Andrew's truck was also filled with fire. Seeing that he was dressed for winter, only his face and hands were badly burned. He jumped out of the truck and put his face to the ground, thinking that there was snow, but he was rubbing his face into the ground. He put dirt and gravel into his face and hands. He wanted the cool of the snow to take away the pain of his burns to his face and hands. He was flown by plane to a hospital in our city, as at that time he was working in another city. Andrew stayed in the medical burn unit for several weeks. He required skin grafts for his hands. When I first saw Andrew, flesh was hanging off his ears, and mouth and his eyes were nothing more than blisters. The doctor was not sure if he even had a nose left.

At the same time, my daughter was downstairs in the ER, seemingly sick unto death. My daughter was seventeen and attempted suicide. On a Friday night she went to bed, and she took a full large bottle of pain medication. I found her the next morning. She was clearly near death. I saw the empty bottle of pills and rushed her to hospital. The doctor told me it was too late and that it would be impossible for her to live. Her liver was destroyed. By the next morning she was able to come home with no side effects. Six months later God told me, "Yes, she was going to die," but He knew she would come to Him, so He saved her life and soul. Praise God!!

At this time, I heard of other painful situations in my marriage. My second husband was also a man who had several affairs. He had on more than one occasion hit me. He would put me down and speak with disrespect. His bad temper caused us to live in fear. He would put his fist through a door and yell and swear. He was a very selfish man - his way or no way.

By the grace of God, my son Andrew recovered from his burns with only scars to his hands, but his face remains beautiful. Initially his face, ears, and hands were so badly burned, his nose was severely damaged, and his ears had hanging flesh. As already mentioned, his closed eyes and lips were nothing more than blisters. His nose was so badly burned the doctor thought he would not even have one. His hands had no flesh on them, and he required skin grafts. Doctors were very surprised at his recovery. God is good and a wonderful healer. My daughter also fully recovered.

My New Life with Jesus Christ

I was now forty-three years old and had come to the end of my own strength. Still, I had not considered surrendering my life to Jesus Christ. My mother had never talked to me about God but had sent us to a Catholic school and church. What I knew about God came from that background. In my day, only the priest could read the Bible. My daughter Linda was in the hospital in the ER, for two days. Normally while she was still in school, she worked part-time at a kitchen and coffee shop. I went to let her boss know she would not be at work for a while since she was in the hospital.

While I was speaking with her Christian boss, I had a thought about myself, "You are going to die, and you're going to commit suicide." I did not know where this thought came from, but I knew that it was true. We went into the back of the shop. Linda's boss asked me if I knew Jesus Christ. I thought that was a silly question, as I felt everyone knew who He was. She told me that if I was the only person on earth, Jesus would have died just for me. I knew Jesus died on the cross for the sins of mankind, but I never knew this as something He would do just for me. She asked me if I would like to make Jesus Christ Lord of my life and ask Him to forgive my sins.

I thought, "What have I got to lose? I do not even want to live anymore." As she led me in prayer, with open eyes, I saw what looked like a Roman lance coming towards me. As it came closer, the lance appeared to be the words she had spoken to me, "Jesus would have died just for you." I watched this lance made up of these words go right into my heart. She also prayed that Jesus would baptize me with joy.

After we prayed, I returned home. As I was sitting at the kitchen table, I had the thought, "Take your cigarettes and put them out of sight." I got up, put them into a kitchen cupboard and returned to my chair. Then I received another thought, "Clean your ashtray." I got up and cleaned my ashtray. I went back to sit. Next it was, "Put your ash tray out of sight." These thoughts were so strong that I was compelled to listen. When I returned to my chair, even more words came to me, "You are not going to smoke, drink, or swear ever again." Then I could feel a fine mist falling on me. I could not see the mist, but I felt wet. That day I stopped smoking, drinking, and swearing.

All of a sudden, I was filled with such joy— joy such as I had never known. At that moment, all fear of my husband left me. For about three months I would look down at my feet to see if they were touching the floor. My joy was so great I thought I was floating. My children wondered what had happened to me. They were used to seeing me sad, angry, or depressed. They knew something big had happened to me. Within a year or so, all my children gave their lives to Jesus Christ. My husband did not know what to make of me. I was no longer afraid and when he would be abusive, it could no longer affect me. He wanted me to be the person he had married, the one who had smoked and sworn. He said, "I command you to be the wife I married."

I laughed out loud, "Never again!" Within the year, I took my children and left the marriage. We went to a women's shelter and from there my new life began. I have not looked back and have never regretted my decision to follow Jesus Christ.

I have been a follower of Jesus Christ for thirty years. There have been many trials and difficult times. But I have never been alone. Jesus has met and cared for all of my large and small needs, as well as performed countless miracles.

In the first year out on my own, I had a bad accident. In my vehicle, I was stopped on a four-lane highway with all lanes blocked and a young man who was not paying attention hit me from behind at 100 km per hour. Usually, both my sons James and John would have been with me. This particular time, only James was with me. Being younger, John always sat in the back, while James sat in the front. I thank God he was not there that day, as the young man put the trunk of my car behind my seat. My son, James, had no injuries, but I had a serious whiplash. At this time, I opened my home to have a New Christian Bible Study. This was a weekly event for me and other new Christians.

One evening, during a study time, my pain was unbearable. My Bible teacher had everyone lay hands on my neck and back.

I felt heat going through my body and was completely healed! After that, there was no more pain from the whiplash.

A few years later, during the winter, my son James had gone out for a skidoo ride and went through a barbed wire fence. The wire had caught his throat and sent him up in the air. He was taken to the hospital. When I arrived, the first thing the doctor said to me was that he should have been decapitated. The doctor said it was a miracle that he survived, but that he would probably never have a voice. He required stitches, but he is alive and well today and has a normal voice. Is that not a miracle?

I was born with one leg shorter than the other and I had a crooked spine. My deformity was very visible. I was not able to walk properly. The doctors wanted to put a rod in my back when I was seventeen, but my mother would not allow it. From the time I was young until I was in my fifties, I suffered with much pain in my lower back. Then I heard about a healing evangelist who had come to a church near my home. I went one evening and when he prayed for me, my right leg grew and lined up with my left leg and my spine went straight! I have never experienced that pain again. Now I was straight and could walk normally. All pain was gone. The doctor measured my legs, and he could see they were the same length, and my spine was now straight as well. All those who knew me saw the changes with their own eyes.

Several years ago, I had company over for supper and had a grand mal seizure. I was rushed to the hospital where medical staff did tests on me. The testing ended up being a two-year ordeal. At the same time, I was having angina attacks and doctors found a tumour on my thyroid. Doctors removed this tumour and I continued to have smaller scale seizures for a year despite medication. They are called petite mal seizures, that is, you do not pass out, but these seizures are more painful, as you are awake while having them.

One night, I forgot to take my angina medication. I knew I was dying. I felt as though I was leaving or sliding out of my body. I never knew how it felt to die, but now I had no fear. As I was sliding out, I said, "Jesus, I am coming home to you." It was as if I heard a voice, "Daughter, it's not your time." I then began to come back up into my body. To be honest, I was disappointed as I was looking forward to heaven.

As I had multiple medical conditions, I could no longer work. I had sold my car to pay off my loan and was living on government assistance for medical leave. During this time, God showed me how He would provide for all my needs. All my friends took me to medical appointments and when I was low on groceries, Jesus would tell them when I needed food. They did not know my need, but God would give them the thought to buy me groceries and they would show up at my door with food. I thank you Linda and Dorothy for doing this for me.

During this time, I attended a Christian Women's Conference. I went up to have prayer for healing While I was waiting for prayer, I started to have a seizure. The woman leading the prayer came over to me and commanded the demon of epilepsy to leave me. She also told the demon of death and angina to leave me. Ever since that prayer in 1999, I have never looked back. I was healed that day from all sickness and delivered from darkness!

I have, over the years as a single mom, had all my needs met. For example, I was once two months behind on my rent. My landlord told me he liked me, as I was a good tenant, but that he needed his rent. I told him I would pray and ask God to supply my need and his. He looked at me in disbelief. Shortly thereafter, my good friends Carrie and Evelyn, who lived out of town, called me. They told me they had been praying for me and wanted to know if I had a need. I told them my situation and between the two of them, they sent five hundred dollars to me. I was a faithful tither and so asked my pastor if the church could help me. He told me they would give me the other five hundred. Praise God, He is always faithful! Within the week, I gave my landlord the $1000 and told him how I received this money. He said, "Your God takes good care of you."

Another time, I lost my glasses. I prayed and asked God to provide me with the money to buy a new pair. The next Sunday, I was at church, and I found a business card for an eyeglass store. The note on the business card said, "Take this card and you will be provided with the glasses you need." When I arrived to purchase my glasses, the sales lady said, "I have never had this happen before. A lady told me to give you any kind of glasses that you want and to also provide you with a continuous line at no charge for bi-focal lenses and sunglasses." The sales lady would not let me know the cost of my choice till I had chosen everything. God was good. Someone paid $600.00 for all of this. Till this day I do not know who blessed me this way. God is so, so good and always faithful.

I enjoy perfume and so when I am around the perfume section of a store, whether I can or cannot afford it, I like to smell the new scents that have come out One time, I could not afford any, but still liked to smell the new ones. As I was walking through the perfume section of a store one day, I was asking Jesus to give me the means to buy some perfume. As I was walking along, a sales lady called me over. She asked me to come and smell a new scent they had just received. I told her it was a lovely scent but that I could not afford it. She said, "I do not know why I am doing this, but you can have this bottle of perfume."

God cares about big things and even the small desires of our hearts.

Another time, I asked God for a fur coat, as Canadian winters are cold, especially in Alberta where I lived. Within a week, my friend Carol, called and said, "Louise, I just received a fur coat from my aunt in the US and it is too small for me. Would you like it?" I then told Carol I had just recently prayed for a fur coat. How quickly God supplied for me! God is good.

Does Jesus care about us and our needs and wants? Surely this proves His Word, He is the God who supplies all of our needs. In the last thirty years that I have been walking with Jesus, I have on more than one occasion, seen my children face sickness, accidents and been near death. Jesus has brought them through it all because He was there all along. He has been faithful to all our needs, even when we are not always faithful. He is still giving me so many promises of wonderful things to come and daily meets my needs and the needs of my family.

In 2015, I was rear ended while sitting at a red light. I experienced whiplash and dizziness. Not long after that I experienced a stroke. I was unable to speak or move my right side and my left was very weak. This has been a long process to recovery. Then in 2018, I was rushed to Emergency with a blood pressure of 289 over 117. The paramedics could do nothing for me as my blood vessels were blowing (ballooning). My stay in the hospital lasted three days. The doctor and other medical staff kept telling me I should be dead. Doctors ran many tests that all turned out normal. Doctors felt sure I must have had another stroke. I told them I am a Christian and my life is in God's hands - if it's not my time nothing can take me out. To my delight, in June of 2018, I was able to start driving again; it was freedom!

January 2019, I experienced pain in my quad while exercising. Some days later my knee gave out and the pain was unbearable. I had a few trips to Emergency and was given different pain medications. After two months of this, I could no longer walk. During this time I went and lived with my daughter. I ended up spending a month in hospital, with all kinds of tests to finally find out I had a pinched nerve in my spine. I was transferred to another hospital for surgery as my L4 and L5 vertebrae were fused. After two more weeks, I was transferred to another hospital for a month of physiotherapy. During that time my amazing daughter, her husband, along with my three sons and granddaughter, packed up my home, had a garage sale, and moved me into my apartment a few weeks later. I continue to believe for complete recovery of my leg and the remaining issues from the stroke. I am so blessed with the family and friends who have helped me in so many ways.

As the years go by, God is taking us from strength to strength and glory to glory. (2 Corinthians 3:18) God's promise to me and all who love and obey Him are found in the following passage:

*When you pass through the waters, I will be with you; and when you pass through the rivers, they will not sweep over you. When you walk through the fire, you will not be burned; the flames will not set you ablaze. For I am the L*ORD*, your God, the Holy One of Israel, your Savior*   Isaiah 43:2-3a (Amplified)

I have read the Word of God and every word is true.

"Come to me, all you who are weary and burdened, and I will give you rest. Take my yoke upon you and learn from me, for I am gentle and humble in heart, and you will find rest for your souls. For my yoke is easy and my burden is light."

Matthew 11:28-30 (NIV)

I have experienced His Word for myself, and God has always been faithful to me. I am not yet complete, but I am nowhere near where I was. I grow daily and trust and obey Him. His promise to me is that He will never leave me or forsake me. I can trust His Word and He is the only One to whom I can say, "Have Your way with me" for He has only good intentions for me.

The greatest call on a child of God is to learn to love like He loves us.

Conclusion

To all the broken and shattered, here is a word from the Lord

"Here is my servant whom I have chosen, the one I love, in whom I delight; I will put my Spirit on him, and he will proclaim justice to the nations. He will not quarrel or cry out; no one will hear his voice in the streets. A bruised reed he will not break, and a smoldering wick he will not snuff out, till he leads justice to victory. In his name the nations will put their hope."
Matthew 12:18-21 (NIV)

It's time for the saints to come to wholeness so we can minister to others who need healing and wholeness with the love of Jesus.

Healing and wholeness can only happen when we allow God to enter our brokenness and places of darkness. Jesus alone is our hope and he is always our more than enough. Jesus came to mankind, willing to lay down His life for all of us. He asks that we be willing to lay down our lives for Him so we can love ourselves as Jesus loves us. God tells us not to love with words alone but with actions and in truth. If we live like this, then we know that we belong to the truth and our hearts will be at rest in God's presence. His timing is always perfect. If we claim to be a child of God but choose to hate and carry any unforgiveness against anyone, then we are still walking in darkness.

Learning to work out our salvation daily is not easy, but if we will persevere, there will be only increase in healing, peace, and joy. If Jesus learned to obey through the things He suffered, it will be the same for us and anyone else who wants to become more like Him. Position, reputation, giftings, finances, spouses, or children must not become an idol, or we will not come to the fullness in Christ. If our desire is that God be first in our hearts, then He alone will bring us to fullness. This process takes time as we allow Jesus to heal our lives. Let God be first, then your family.

We need God, fathers, mothers, grandfathers, grandmothers, brothers, sisters, aunts, uncles, cousins, and friends loving and caring for one another. It is time to love one another according to the word of God. Only love and truth can bring transformation to the wounded soul. Again, the foundation of any society is God, marriage, and the family. Many of us have not known this family support but, rest assured, God has people ready and willing to love and be His hands and feet to bring healing.

I have known many Christians who love God, and their desire is to go deeper in their relationship with God. Some have told me that after years of prayer, ministry, and attending many conferences, they have become discouraged. They are still looking for healing that never seems to come their way. Sadly, some give up and leave the fellowship of believers.

The testimonies in this book are proof that there is hope for the broken and shattered souls that are searching for their long-awaited healing.

The Bible is full of scriptures that speak to those who have suffered trauma and abuses of every kind. Only Jesus can heal the broken hearts of those who are still trapped in pain and sorrow.

I will lead the blind by ways they have not known, along unfamiliar paths I will guide them; I will turn the darkness into light before them and make the rough places smooth. These are the things I will do; I will not forsake them.
                                              Isaiah 42:16 (NIV)

But this is a people plundered and looted, all of them trapped in pits or hidden away in prisons. They have become plunder, with no one to rescue them; they have been made loot, with no one to say, "Send them back."   Isaiah 42:22 (NIV)

We all know people who love their sin or darkness and will never change.

Jesus tells us,

"Come to God through the narrow gate, because the wide gate and broad path is the way that leads to destruction—nearly everyone chooses that crowded road! The narrow gate and the difficult way leads to eternal life—so few even find it!"   Matthew 7:13-14 (TPT)

There is really nothing that comes easy in life except receiving the free gift of salvation that Jesus paid at the Cross. The person who truly wants to change and find healing and wholeness in life is the one willing to change and do the work, in order to walk in freedom in Christ.

Healing and wholeness can only be accomplished if we are willing to come to Jesus. He is the only way, the truth, and the life.

Jesus answered, "I am the way and the truth and the life. No one comes to the Father except through me."
                                              John 14:6 (NIV)

Commentary on Noah's Ark

By Michelle McDonald

Healing is available in the Genesis chapters 6 to 8 flood story. God is making healing available, as He did through the flood to individuals, churches, peoples, and nations today just as He did when the ark came to rest on Mount Ararat "...on the 17th day of the 7th month." (Genesis 8:4)

The Problem

The earth was depraved and putrid in God's sight, and the land was filled with violence (desecration, infringement, outrage, assault, and lust for power). And God looked upon the world and saw how degenerate, debased, and vicious it was, for all humanity had corrupted their way upon the earth and lost their true direction. Genesis 6:11-12 (Amplified)

For the individual, family, church, or nation.

But this is a people plundered and looted, all of them trapped in pits or hidden away in prisons. They have become plunder, with no one to rescue them; they have been made loot, with no one to say, "Send them back." Isaiah 42:22 (NIV)

The Healing

In Genesis 6 and 7 God sent the flood. The number 8 represents new beginnings, and it is the healing process that God performed in Genesis 8 that we are interested in.

AND GOD [earnestly] remembered Noah and every living thing and all the animals that were with him in the ark;
Genesis 8:1a (Amplified)

There comes a day that is God's appointed time for healing to start in your life. The people who can help you are in place, you are willing to face whatever is needed for healing to take place and you have the freedom, time, or responsibility to do it.

... and God made a wind blow over the land, and the waters sank down and abated.   *Genesis 8:1b (Amplified)*

God sends His Holy Spirit over the area that needs healing and starts the healing process by exposing the damaged areas to the light. As you agree with the truth that the Spirit reveals, repenting when necessary and continuing in forgiveness and submission to Jesus as Lord, more and more of the damaged areas will come to light.

Also the fountains of the deep and the windows of the heavens were closed, the gushing rain from the sky was checked, And the waters receded from the land continually.
Genesis 8:2-3a (Amplified)

There comes a time in the above-mentioned healing process, where God closes the fountains of the deep. The fountains represent the doors through which the works of the world, the devil, and your flesh attack you through the iniquity of your lineage, as well as the land. The fountains also represent the doors that your own sins have opened up. Dealing with these doors is in itself a process.

Checking the gushing rain from the sky means that God checks the curses and issues coming at you. This should bring breakthrough into prosperity in adversities and repeating problems in your life. This means much more than monetary wealth, in that your body, soul and spirit are prosperous. But it is not so much a removal of all the bad things as a closing of the doors that the curses and issues get through to get to you as you enter into the shalom peace of God. This is a process.

On the seventeenth day of the seventh month the ark came to rest on the mountains of Ararat [in Armenia]. And the waters continued to diminish until the tenth month; on the first day of the tenth month the tops of the high hills were seen.
Genesis 8:4-5 (Amplified)

Yes, it usually takes time for the waters of all the putrid stuff such as hurt, unforgiveness, and other soul damage to recede.

At the end of [another] forty days Noah opened a window of the ark which he had made and sent forth a raven, which kept going to and fro until the waters were dried up from the land.

Then he sent forth a dove to see if the waters had decreased from the surface of the ground. But the dove found no resting-place on which to roost, and she returned to him to the ark, for the waters were [yet] on the face of the whole land. So he put forth his hand and drew her to him into the ark. He waited another seven days and again sent forth the dove out of the ark. And the dove came back to him in the evening, and behold, in her mouth was a newly sprouted and freshly plucked olive leaf! So Noah knew that the waters had subsided from the land. Then he waited another seven days and sent forth the dove, but she did not return to him anymore.

Genesis 8:6-12 (Amplified)

There is a partnership with God that happens throughout the healing process. God is the Alpha, Omega, Beginning and the End, and we are God's workmanship created in Christ Jesus to do good works, which God prepared in advance for us to do. (Ephesians 2:10) We have freedom of choice and the more we cooperate with God and His plans for us, the faster and easier it will go. Faith without works is dead. (James 2:26)

Note that the raven is one of the two smartest birds in the world and if there is something to find, a raven will find it. Maybe that's why God chose a raven to find food for Elijah. Note that the dove is a homing bird and Noah and his family needed a home. It is also a symbol of the Holy Spirit and so these two birds being released mark a new work of restoration, where Noah was able to have a closer partnership with God. As we are healed, we can be more and more intimate with God, and this brings more capabilities and fruitfulness. The result is more filling of the Holy Spirit, and we fight the darkness instead we build a home, grow, create, and start bringing light to others.

Note also that the dove brought the leaf of an olive tree after God had destroyed every living thing that was upon the face of the earth. (Genesis 7:23) A creative miracle! There are deep implications pertaining to the olive tree: the olive leaf and healing, the olive branch and peace, olive oil was used in the temple as part of worship.

There was only one quality of olive oil that could be used in the temple. The first and highest quality press of oil is made from the weight of the olives left overnight in the press, which pushes out the olive oil out without hands. The Hebrew word Gethsemane refers to the olive oil press with high quantities of this pure, high-quality oil made without hands that came from Jesus when He was pressed. Gethsemane is also a Greek word that refers to a dark ravine or valley, like the Valley of the Shadow of Death in Psalm 23:4.

What kind of oil are you producing as you are going through this extremely difficult and pressing time in your life? I exhort you to be filled with the Holy Spirit and produce the pure oil of Christ through this time because you are co-heir with Him and co-labouring with Him to build God's temple in you so that you can fulfill God's destiny for you with fruitfulness! Enjoy the rainbow of God's promise that He will not make you go through this again and the unlimited increase of His favour and blessings upon you. (Genesis 9:8-12)

Other Books by the Same Author

YOU'RE ALL A BUNCH OF PEAS
© 2014 by Louise Franck

Publisher: Word Alive Press (May 8, 2016)
ISBN: 978-1486607310

Tragically, the world is full of broken souls. We have all said and done things we wish we could change. **You're All a Bunch of Peas** gives the answer for healing and wholeness in our lives.

I will lead the blind by ways they have not known, along unfamiliar paths I will guide them; I will turn the darkness into light before them and make the rough places smooth. These are the things I will do; I will not forsake them.
                                                            Isaiah 42:16 (NIV)

About the Author: As minister of **Hope for the Broken Soul Ministry**, Sherwood Park, Alberta, Canada, Louise Franck offers intercessory prayer for those who come looking for spiritual direction. Lay minister for ten years in a small church in Sherwood Park, Louise is presently writing her third book.

You can buy ***You're All a Bunch of Peas*** here:

https://www.amazon.ca/YOURE-BUNCH-PEAS-Louise-Franck/dp/1486607314/ref=tmm_pap_swatch_0?_encoding=UTF8&qid=1590600150&sr=1-1

Recommended Ministries

The Summit Church - Edmonton

8717 50 Street NW

Edmonton, AB, Canada T6B 1E7

https://www.thesummitchurch.ca/

Senior Pastor: Chris Mathis

Bethel Church

933 College View Drive

Redding, California 9633, USA

https://www.bethel.com/

Senior Pastor: Bill Johnson

Recommended Material

Your Body His Temple: God's Plan for Achieving Emotional Wholeness

Life Today Video: https://lifetoday.org/video/your-body-his-temple-series-26/

By: PhD, Dr. Caroline Leaf, Marty Copeland, Janet Maccaro

https://drleaf.com/

Changes That Heal
(The Four Shifts That Make Everything Better... And That Anyone Can Do)

https://www.drcloud.com/books/changes-that-heal

By: Dr. Henry Cloud

https://www.drcloud.com/

The Life Model: Living from the Heart Jesus Gave You, Living from the Heart Jesus Gave You

By: James G Friesen, PhD. James Wilder, Anne M. Bierling M.A., Rick Koepcke, M.A., Marybeth Pool, M.A.

https://www.amazon.ca/Life-Model-Essentials-Christian-Revised/dp/0967435749

Time to Defeat the Devil: Strategies to Win the Spiritual War

By: Chuck Pierce

https://www.amazon.ca/Time-Defeat-Devil-Strategies-Spiritual-ebook/dp/B0053HJ1NM/ref=sr_1_2?dchild=1&keywords=time+to+defeat+the+devil&qid=1632342584&sr=8-2

Summit Global Publishing Ltd.

In December 2020, Tracy Belford received a vision from the Lord to open a publishing company. The purpose was to share the word of the Lord that was coming out of The Summit Edmonton Church. She was inspired by Romans 10:17 (NKJV) *"So then faith comes by hearing, and hearing by the word of God."*

Tracy believed that God was sharing so much wisdom and revelation within her church that it needed to be shared on a larger scale to increase the faith of many. To date, she has published two books: *Living in Devotion*, a collaboration of The Summit Edmonton Church leadership, and *Hope for the Broken* by Louise Franck.

Upcoming books include:

- *Just Eat the Cake*
- *Signs, Wonders, and Miracles* - Testimonies from The Summit
- as well as additional devotional books.

Summit Global Publishing Ltd. continues to accept manuscripts from individuals within the Summit Global family. To submit a manuscript, please email tracy@thesummitchurch.ca.

Made in the USA
Monee, IL
04 November 2021